A Trainer's Guide
to
Caring for Preschool Children

Second Edition

Derry G. Koralek
Debra D. Al-Salam
Diane Trister Dodge

**Cover design by
Ayesha Husain**

**Cover illustrations by
Jennifer Barrett O'Connell**

**P.O. Box 42243
Washington, DC 20015**

Published by

Teaching Strategies, Inc.
P.O. Box 42243
Washington, DC 20015

Distributed by

Gryphon House, Inc.
P.O. Box 207
Beltsville, MD 20704-0207

ISBN: 1-879537-28-1

Library of Congress Catalog Card Number: 96-061877

Acknowledgments

Caring for Preschool Children and this *Trainer's Guide* are based on materials originally developed by the authors for the U.S. Navy and U.S. Army Child Development Services. Carolee Callen, Head of the Navy Child Development Services Branch, originally conceived of the idea of a standardized, self-instructional training program for child care staff. M.-A. Lucas, Chief of Child Development Services in the U.S. Army, funded an adaptation of the training program to support CDA training in Army child development centers. We are indebted to these two individuals, their Headquarters staff, and the staff at Navy and Army child development centers who reviewed all drafts of the materials developed under this contract and provided us with constructive and helpful suggestions that greatly improved the program.

Contents

Introduction

A sound approach to staff development is an essential factor in achieving a high-quality program. *Caring for Preschool Children* offers comprehensive, competency-based training for teachers in a variety of early childhood settings. Because the program is self-instructional, teachers can use it at their own pace, as time permits. This approach allows for teacher autonomy in completing the training. But that autonomy also means trainers must play a very active role in advising teachers during the training and in tracking their progress. The trainer's central role is to conduct objective observations of teachers working with children, model appropriate practices, and provide feedback and support. Trainers review and make judgments about the appropriateness of teachers' responses in the learning activities. Trainers also assess the knowledge and competence teachers gain as they complete each module.

The training program consists of a two-volume set for staff and this *Trainer's Guide.*

Caring for Preschool Children Training Program

For Staff:

For Trainers:

Contents

The Context

Overview

Overseeing the Program

Leading Group Training

Assessing Progress

   Knowledge Assessments

   Competency Assessments

Planning and Training Forms

1

A Trainer's Guide to Caring for Preschool Children, 2nd Edition has five chapters and six appendices.

Chapter I, A Context for Staff Development—Making Training Count, discusses current efforts to establish an organized system for professional development. It describes the components of such a system and shows how this training program promotes career development and program improvement.

Chapter II, An Overview of *Caring for Preschool Children,* describes the training materials, explains the content addressed through the modules, and shows how the training approach adheres to principles of adult learning.

Chapter III, Overseeing the Training Program, provides an overview of the trainer's role in introducing the training program, completing the Orientation, and providing feedback to teachers as they complete each section of the modules. It also describes what teachers and trainers do to complete each module and offers suggested strategies for extending learning.

Chapter IV, Leading Group Training Sessions, is targeted to trainers who will implement the training through group settings such as workshops, seminars, or college courses. It describes training techniques, logistics, facilitating group training sessions, and methods for evaluating training. A sample outline is provided for leading a series of group training sessions on Module 10, Guidance.

Chapter V, Assessing Each Teacher's Progress, offers guidance on administering and conducting the knowledge and competency assessments, and scoring and discussing the results. The knowledge assessments and competency assessment observation forms are at the end of this chapter.

The appendices include:

A. Planning Form for Group Training Sessions, used by trainers in group settings;

B. Answer Sheets for Knowledge Assessments, used to score knowledge assessments;

C. Tracking Forms to monitor individual and program progress;

D. Training Record to document what, when, how, and by whom training is provided;

E. Certificate of Completion, awarded to teachers who complete the training program; and

F. Publishers and Distributors of Resources, as described in the Orientation to *Caring for Preschool Children.*

Chapter I

A Context for Staff Development—Making Training Count

Chapter I

A Context for Staff Development—Making Training Count

This chapter describes:

- The importance of ensuring that training is part of an organized system

- The components of an organized system of professional development

- Linking training to professional development and program improvement

---

Caring for Preschool Children is one in a series of comprehensive, competency-based training programs for center-based staff and family child care providers working with children from birth through school age. The training program includes this *Trainer's Guide* and a two-volume set for teachers. Your decision to use *Caring for Preschool Children* represents a commitment to the professional development of one or more individuals who work with children three to five years old in a center-based setting. This commitment requires more than simply selecting a high-quality training program.

Effective training experiences exist within a context. Just as curriculum for young children is not simply a collection of activities, a series of workshops alone do not lead to professional growth. The training you provide using *Caring for Preschool Children* must fit into a well-established system of professional development.

The Need for an Organized System

Early childhood education, as defined by the National Association for Early Childhood Education (NAEYC), includes: "any part- or full-day group program in a center, school, or home that serves children from birth through age eight, including children with special developmental and learning needs."[1]

The field of early childhood education is broad and allows for multiple entry points. Some members of our field enter from colleges and graduate schools with advanced degrees in teaching. Some begin preparing in high school vocational programs. Still others enter the field with no professional preparation and gain professional knowledge and skills entirely on the job. The early childhood field, therefore, includes a diversity of roles in a variety of settings and must accommodate many different kinds of preparation.

As a result, many individuals working in early childhood settings do not have a recognized credential or degree. The likelihood exists that this number will increase as Head Start expands and the need for full-time child care increases. For this reason, individuals representing a range of organizations are coming together to design comprehensive professional development systems.

---

[1] "NAEYC Position Statement: A Conceptual Framework for Early Childhood Professional Development," *Young Children* (Washington, DC: National Association for the Education of Young Children, November, 1994).

In 1988, only one state, Delaware, was involved in a concerted effort to create a state-wide career development system. By 1996, the number of states involved in similar initiatives rose to 47.[2] This remarkable increase represents a growing awareness of the diversity of our field and consensus on the components that must be in place in order to achieve a comprehensive career development system. It further demonstrates that professional development takes place when teachers participate in an organized, high-quality system which focuses on the acquisition of specific skills and knowledge, leads to a certificate or credit towards a degree, and results in improved compensation and benefits.

Components of a Professional Development System

Leading organizations in early childhood education, including NAEYC, the Center for Career Development in Early Care and Education at Wheelock College, and the National Center for the Early Childhood Work Force (NCECW) helped to identify the components of a professional development system. These organizations are also providing technical assistance and resources to state groups as they design their own systems.

As you consider how to use *Caring for Preschool Children* in your work, you'll need to make sure that all training experiences fit into a career development plan for each teacher who participates. Take the time to learn about the system that is being established in your state, as well as what is happening on a national level. Hopefully you will find that several key components of an organized professional development system are in place. These components are described below.

Agreement on a Core Body of Knowledge and Competencies

Every profession defines a specialized body of knowledge and competencies that are expected of all members of that profession. Training experiences—regardless of where they take place—should address the core curriculum that defines the early childhood profession.

In designing systems of professional development, most states have adopted or based their core curriculum on the eight competency areas outlined by The Council for Early Childhood Professional Recognition. This core body of knowledge and competencies recognizes that effective teachers of young children:

- demonstrate an understanding of child development and can apply this knowledge in practice;

- observe and assess children's behavior in planning and individualizing teaching practices and curriculum;

- establish and maintain a safe and healthy environment for children;

- plan and implement developmentally appropriate curriculum that advances all areas of children's learning and development, including social, emotional, intellectual, and physical competence;

---

[2] Azer, Sheri L., Karen L. Caprano, and Kimberly A. Elliott, *Working Toward Making a Career of It: A Profile of Career Development Initiatives in 1996* (The Center for Career Development in Early Care and Education, Wheelock College, Boston, MA, 1996).

- establish supportive relationships with children and implement developmentally appropriate techniques of guidance and group management;

- establish and maintain positive and productive relationships with families;

- support the development and learning of individual children, recognizing that children are best understood in the context of family, culture, and society; and

- demonstrate an understanding of the early childhood profession and make a commitment to professionalism.

These eight competencies provide a blueprint for individual professional development and a way to assess progress. They serve as the content for all training experiences. *Caring for Preschool Children* addresses all of these competencies by organizing content around the 13 functional areas as defined by The Council for Early Childhood Professional Recognition.

A Training Approval System

A second component of a comprehensive system of professional development is a training approval system to ensure that all training experiences meet quality standards and lead to professional development. A training approval system should include procedures for reviewing and recognizing workshops and conferences as eligible for continuing education units and college or graduate credit; categorizing college courses in terms of their relevance to licensing requirements and credentialing programs; and ensuring that training experiences meet requirements for specific training levels and topic areas.

In developing a training approval system, many states have found it helpful to follow a set of principles of effective professional development. As defined by NAEYC,[3] effective professional development experiences:

- are part of an ongoing process allowing staff to continually incorporate and apply new knowledge and skills related to working with children and families;

- are grounded in a sound theoretical and philosophical base and structured as a coherent and systematic program;

- are responsive to an individual's background, experiences, and current role;

- allow staff to see clear linkages between theory and practice;

- use interactive, hands-on approaches that encourage staff to learn from one another;

- contribute to positive self-esteem by acknowledging the skills and resources staff bring to the training process;

---

[3] "NAEYC Position Statement: A Conceptual Framework for Early Childhood Professional Development," *Young Children* (Washington, DC: National Association for the Education of Young Children, November, 1994).

- provide opportunities for application and reflection and allow staff to be observed and receive feedback about what they have learned; and

- encourage staff to take responsibility for planning their own professional development program.

The training approach used in *Caring for Preschool Children* reflects and builds on these principles.

Many states are establishing criteria for individuals who offer training as part of the career development system. This criteria may include evidence of the following:

- knowledge, education, and experience in early childhood education and child development, including areas of specialization such as special needs, which qualify them to teach the content of the class;

- knowledge of how adults learn, including demonstrated sensitivity to individual differences and learning styles;

- sensitivity to cultural and linguistic diversity and to one's own cultural biases;

- understanding of the early childhood profession and a commitment to professionalism; and

- knowledge of state and local regulations and requirements for programs and staff.

Organizations that offer training for staff—child care agencies, Head Start programs, resource and referral agencies, Child and Adult Care Food Programs, Departments of Recreation, colleges, universities, schools—may also be required to meet criteria established by the state. Such criteria may include ensuring that all their trainers meet established qualifications, that training offered meets the requirements for licensing, certification, credentialing, or a degree in early childhood education, and that the content of training is based on accepted theories and practices in early childhood education and addresses the core competencies identified by the early childhood profession. Additionally, organizations must set up a system for documenting the training provided (e.g., transcripts, certificates of attendance) and maintain a permanent record of attendance at these sessions.

A Personnel Registry

A third essential component of a professional development system is a centralized tracking system to document all training completed by every individual in the profession. Documentation of training can include official transcripts from a college or university, a certificate of participation from an organization providing training which is signed by the trainer or a representative from the sponsoring group, or an official form provided at a conference or training session, with appropriate safeguards to ensure validation of each person's participation. Forms used for documentation, such as those included in Appendix D of this *Trainer's Guide*, become part of the individual's permanent record. Documentation must include the following information:

- the participant's name;

- the title of the workshop, course, or seminar, and the competency area addressed; date(s) of training;

- total number of hours of training completed, including designation of clock hours or credit hours (and the number of clock hours which constitute one credit hour); and

- signature or stamp of instructor or program administrator.

A permanent registry for training records is essential to achieving the goal of professional development for several reasons. Many states have staff training requirements built into licensing requirements. Centers must keep these records but they should also be maintained in a centralized place. A number of colleges and universities are considering ways to arrange college credit for training experiences being offered by certified trainers that address the profession's standards but are not part of the regular college program. Full documentation of these training experiences will be essential for career development.

Linking Training to Professional Development and Program Improvement

In the past several years, an increasing body of research has identified a link between training, program quality, and positive outcomes for children. The National Child Care Staffing Study suggests that accredited centers provide higher-than-average-quality services. "The accredited centers had better-compensated teachers with more formal education and specialized early childhood training, provided better benefits and working conditions, and maintained lower rates of turnover."[4]

As described above, tremendous progress has been made in designing the kind of comprehensive systems that are needed to enhance the quality of programs serving young children and in promoting the professional development of those who work in these programs. However, most state regulations still fall far short of ensuring that programs meet standards of quality that all children need to thrive. Welfare reform poses new challenges to our profession as some states consider lowering standards for programs and staff qualifications in order to expand child care services.

Caring for Preschool Children can be an effective tool for promoting professional growth and program improvement. The 13 modules in the training program can be applied to obtaining a Child Development Associate (CDA) Credential or program accreditation as described below.

A CDA Credential: The First Step in Professional Development

The Child Development Associate National Credentialing Program is a major effort to provide early childhood educators with a credential based on demonstrated competency. The program began in 1971 with the goal of improving the quality of early childhood education by improving, evaluating, and recognizing the

---

[4] Whitebrook, M., "NAEYC Accreditation As an Indicator of Program Quality: What Research Tells Us," *NAEYC Accreditation: A Decade of Learning and the Years Ahead,* S. Bredekamp and B. Willer, Editors (Washington, DC: NAEYC, 1996), p. 35.

competence of individuals who work with children from birth to age five in center-based and family child care settings.

The Council for Early Childhood Professional Recognition establishes the policies and sets the standards for the credentialing program and awards the CDA Credential. The Council awards a CDA Credential to teachers and family child care providers who demonstrate competence in caring for young children. To date, nearly 85,000 early care and education workers have received a CDA Credential.

There are two routes to obtaining a CDA Credential: Direct Assessment and the Professional Preparation Program. To apply through Direct Assessment, a Candidate must document completion of 120 contact hours of training with no less than ten hours in each of the eight subject areas defined by the profession. Formal training can be provided by training specialists, Head Start or child care agencies, colleges, vocational/technical schools, or resource and referral agencies, and must cover the specific subject areas outlined by the Council. Completion of the 13 modules in *Caring for Preschool Children* will enable teachers to meet or exceed the Council's training requirements. (A sample form for documenting contact hours can be found in Appendix D.)

Teachers applying for a Credential are responsible for developing a Professional Resource File, which is a collection of documents to use in working with children and families. The learning activities in *Caring for Preschool Children* include many opportunities for teachers to document work and collect materials that can be included in their Professional Resource File.

Direct Assessment also requires teachers to complete a written and oral assessment and be observed working directly with children. The knowledge and competency assessments used after completing each module will help teachers prepare for the CDA assessments.

In the second route to obtaining a CDA Credential, the Council will arrange for teachers to enter a college-level Professional Preparation Program, which offers training and assessment using the Council's curriculum, *Essentials*. There are three phases in the CDA Professional Preparation Program: field work, instructional course work, and evaluation.

To keep up-to-date on the process for obtaining a CDA Credential, contact The Council for Early Childhood Professional Recognition at (800) 424-4310.

Program Improvement Through Accreditation

Program accreditation is a voluntary approach for recognizing and promoting high-quality programs serving young children. The accreditation process can be a powerful motivator for everyone working at the site to come together and work towards program improvement.

Accreditation begins with an extensive self-study process focusing on established criteria. All program staff and parents complete forms to evaluate the program and identify areas where improvement is needed. Many of the trainers and directors who use *Caring for Preschool Children* review the results of this self-assessment process when selecting the modules to introduce first to teachers. For example, if a program does not meet the standards for ensuring children's health, all teachers can begin with Module 2, Healthy, and discuss each learning activity as a group.

When program staff feel they have met the criteria, the accrediting organization sets up a site-visit from a validator who verifies the accuracy of the program's self-assessment. The validated self-assessment is reviewed by a commission or board which has the power to grant accreditation for a specified period of years, or to defer accreditation and make recommendations on areas that must be improved first. Three national systems now exist for center-based programs.[5]

The National Academy of Early Childhood Programs, a division of NAEYC, administers a national, voluntary, professionally sponsored accreditation system for all types of preschools, kindergartens, child care centers, and school-age child care programs. Since 1985, approximately 4,500 programs in all fifty states have achieved NAEYC accreditation and an additional 8,000 programs are in the self-study process.

> National Academy of Early Childhood Programs/NAEYC
> 1509 16th Street, N.W.
> Washington, DC 20036   (202) 232-8777 or (800) 424-2460

The National Early Childhood Program Accreditation (NECPA) is an independent voluntary accreditation program developed with the National Child Care Association, the largest organization of proprietary child care professionals. Since 1992, the NECPA has accredited 44 centers in ten states.

> The National Early Childhood Program Accreditation Commission
> 1023 Railroad Street
> Conyers, GA   (800) 543-7161

National Accreditation Council for Early Childhood Professional Personnel and Programs is a national, non-profit organization that supports private and ecumenical, licensed, center-based early childhood programs. The organization is sponsored by the Child Care Institute of America. Since 1992, the Council has accredited 80 programs in five states.

> The National Early Childhood Program Accreditation
> Cleveland Park Station
> PO Box 9518
> Washington, DC 20016-9518

Using the Training Program in College Courses

Caring for Preschool Children is used as the text for a range of courses offered through community colleges and four-year institutions. The chart on the following page shows how the modules might be grouped into a series of courses. This model is based on 12 credit hours that would lead to fulfillment of the requirements for a credential, accreditation, or college credit towards a degree. Another way that colleges might award credit is to offer a series of one-credit-hour classes based on the modules, thus giving teachers a range of choices for augmenting their training experiences. See Chapter IV, Leading Group Training Sessions, for additional guidance on adapting the training approach for group settings.

---

[5] Stoney Associates, "Accreditation as a Quality Improvement Strategy" in *Building and Maintaining an Effective Child Care/Early Education System in Your State*, A collection of issue briefs by national organizations whose major focus is on early education/child care issues, 1996, pp. 20-22.

Using *Caring for Preschool Children* for
Professional Development and Program Improvement

Course Title	*Caring for Preschool Children* Modules	Clock Hours	CDA Subject Areas Addressed	Center Accreditation
Establishing the Environment	1-Safe 2-Healthy 3-Learning Environment	12 12 14	Planning a safe, healthy, learning environment	Safety, Health, Nutrition, Physical Environment
Child Growth and Development: Cognitive and Physical	4-Physical 5-Cognitive 6-Communication 7-Creative	10 10 10 10	Steps to advance children's physical and intellectual development Principles of child growth and development	Curriculum, Interactions among Staff and Children
Child Growth and Development: Social and Emotional	8-Self 9-Social 10-Guidance	11 11 16	Positive ways to support children's social and emotional development Principles of child growth and development	Interactions among Staff and Children
Introduction to the Early Childhood Profession	11-Families 12-Program Management 13-Professionalism	10 20 10	Strategies to establish productive relationships with families Strategies to manage an effective program operation Maintaining a commitment to professionalism Observing and recording children's behavior	Staff-Parent Interaction, Staff Qualifications and Development, Evaluation, Administration
Applied Early Childhood Practices (Lab or Practicum)	This course would include observations of each student's application of material presented in class and provide individualized support and feedback.	16	Observations by an Advisor are part of the CDA credentialing process.	Site validator visit

Chapter II

An Overview of Caring for Preschool Children

Chapter II

An Overview of Caring for Preschool Children

This chapter describes:

- The training materials

- The content of the training

- The training approach

The Training Materials

Caring for Preschool Children is comprised of 13 modules in a two-volume set. Volume I includes the Orientation and Modules 1 through 6; Volume II contains Modules 7 through 13. The Orientation provides a summary of the training content and process, a glossary of professional terms, definitions of the 13 functional areas of the Child Development Associate (CDA) Competency Standards, and a bibliography of recommended resources for early childhood professionals. The Orientation ends with a self-assessment, which lists for each module, three major skills used by competent teachers. Teachers use the results of the self-assessment to develop a module completion plan. This plan lists the first three modules the teacher plans to work on with target completion dates, and a tentative schedule for completing the entire training program.

Each module is organized in the same way. The **overview** introduces the topics and major skills to be addressed in the module, provides concrete examples of teachers applying these skills, and allows teachers to relate the topic to personal experiences. A **pre-training assessment** lists specific skills competent teachers should possess in each area. Five to six **learning activities** follow. Each learning activity has several pages of text, followed by instructions for teachers to apply the information to their work with children and families. At the end of each module comes **summarizing your progress**, an opportunity to reflect on learning and skill development, **answer sheets**, and a **glossary**. The chart that follows outlines the organizational framework used for each module.

How Each Module Is Organized

Section	Description
Overview	An introduction to the topics addressed in the module and definition of three major skills teachers must have An opportunity to relate the topic to personal experiences (e.g., Your Own Safety)
Pre-Training Assessment	A checklist of the relevant skills used by competent teachers
Learning Activities (5 to 6 per module)	Information about a specific topic and an opportunity to apply knowledge while working with children and families
Summarizing Your Progress	A format for reviewing the knowledge and skills gained by completing all of the learning activities in the module
Answer Sheets	Suggested responses to learning activities
Glossary	Definitions of the terms used in the module

The Training Content

Caring for Preschool Children is designed so that teachers can gain the knowledge and skills needed to plan and implement developmentally appropriate programs for children ages 3 through 5. We use the term "teachers" to include classroom teachers and assistants, college students, volunteers, and others who work with preschool children and families in child development programs such as Head Start, and in private and public child care centers.

The content of the training program focuses on the 13 functional areas of the CDA Competency Standards. Each module addresses the knowledge and skills related to a functional area: Safe, Healthy, Learning Environment, Physical, Cognitive, Communication, Creative, Self, Social, Guidance, Families, Program Management, and Professionalism. (See the Orientation in *Caring for Preschool Children* for definitions of each functional area.)

The following skills and concepts are repeated and reinforced throughout the modules.

- **Competent teachers can apply their knowledge of child development.** They use what they know about preschool children to plan for each child and for the group. The first learning activity in Modules 1 through 10 summarizes the typical characteristics of preschool children and describes how they are related to the topics addressed in the module. In addition, many learning activities include information about child development and opportunities to apply this knowledge on the job.

- **Competent teachers establish strong partnerships with families.** This training program acknowledges parents as the prime educators of their children. In addition to completing Module 11, Families, teachers involve families as they carry out and discuss learning activities in other modules. The modules emphasize the importance of reflecting ethnicity, cultures, languages, and families in all aspects of the program.

- **Competent teachers conduct systematic, objective observations.** Observations allow teachers to learn about each child, measure children's progress, and evaluate program effectiveness. Information gathered through regular, systematic observations helps teachers learn about each child's needs, skills, interests, and individual characteristics. This information is shared with families and is used to plan for the group and for individual children.

- **Competent teachers offer an individualized program.** This topic is addressed in depth in Module 12, Program Management. In addition, it is reinforced through many learning activities. Teachers observe individual children and report on what they learn about each child. They use what they have learned to make decisions about introducing new materials, rearranging the environment, tailoring their interactions, or sharing information with families.

- **Competent teachers take time to reflect on their practices.** Reflection is an important part of most learning activities. Teachers plan, implement, then report on and evaluate what took place. They describe how they might change an activity if offered again, what materials they could provide to help a child gain specific skills, what props to offer that could enhance children's play, or ways to make the environment safer for children.

The Training Approach

The training approach combines self-instruction with support and feedback from a trainer. We use the term "trainer" to refer to a center director, mentor teacher, college instructor, or any other individual who can observe teachers, provide feedback on their performance, and guide their continued learning and professional development. Trainers introduce the program to teachers and offer ongoing guidance and support. Teachers apply new information immediately while working with children. As a result, teachers can see how their professional development affects children and contributes to overall program improvement efforts.

Throughout the training process, trainers observe teachers as they work with children and provide feedback and support during one-on-one and group training sessions. They address individual learning styles by offering additional resources and approaches and by suggesting strategies for extending learning. As teachers complete each module, trainers assess their knowledge and competence and track their progress.

Key Features

The training approach incorporates several key features that are critical to its success.

Training is individualized. *Caring for Preschool Children* can be used by new or experienced teachers to increase their knowledge and understanding of preschool children and developmentally appropriate practice. The self-assessment and pre-training assessments are designed to acknowledge and build on each teacher's existing skills and knowledge. The module completion plan allows teachers and trainers to determine individual schedules for completing the modules. The learning activities invite teachers to make choices—which child to observe, which activity to plan and implement, when to use a checklist, what part of the environment to assess and improve. Teachers are encouraged to use critical thinking and reflect on their own performance. They participate in the process of determining whether they are ready for the assessment process.

Teachers receive ongoing feedback based on regular, systematic observations. While much of the training involves self-instruction, the role of the trainer is critical to application of knowledge. Trainers observe teachers working with children, give feedback based on these observations, model appropriate practices, and discuss completed learning activities.

The training involves hands-on learning. Most of the learning activities require teachers to develop skills while applying knowledge on the job. Teachers develop, implement, and evaluate plans with colleagues. They develop partnerships with families, use observation notes to individualize their programs, and complete checklists to identify and address problems.

The training is competency-based. Knowledge and competency assessments are built into the training process. The assessments acknowledge each teacher's growth and learning and provide a sense of closure before beginning the next module.

Motivating Adult Learners

The training design and approach for *Caring for Preschool Children* reflects an understanding of adult learning principles. Most adults are self-directed and want to be responsible for their own learning. How much they get out of training depends on how important the content is to them, how much effort they put into the learning process, and whether they integrate and use what they learn. Trainers need to consider what motivates adults to learn and how principles of adult learning theory can be applied to training.

For most adults, motivation for learning is closely related to whether they can **immediately apply the knowledge and skills being addressed.** They want to know what they will be learning so they can determine whether it is useful. This training program defines clear objectives in the self-assessment, the pre-training assessments, and at the beginning of each learning activity, so teachers can clearly see what they will be learning and how it relates to their work with children.

Adults view job-related learning as a means to an end, not an end in itself. They are motivated to participate in training that allows them to **develop or improve specific job-related skills**. The learning activities in *Caring for Preschool Children* address this motivator because they are completed on the job.

Time is a limited and valuable investment for working adults. They have more positive attitudes towards training when they believe the **time invested is well-spent**. The knowledge and skills gained through this training program will help teachers become more effective in their work with children. Trainers can reinforce this motivator by pointing out to teachers how their increased skills and knowledge are benefiting children.

Strong secondary factors relating to an adult's motivation to learn are to **increase their self-esteem and enjoyment of work**. This training program acknowledges and builds on what teachers already know. It includes opportunities for teachers to feel successful and competent as they complete learning activities, modules, and the assessment process. Teachers who know they are competent tend to enjoy their work and want to continue learning.

According to many studies, motivation increases with **recognition for achievements, respect for the individual as a person,** and **participation in planning and decision making**. The assessment process in *Caring for Preschool Children* provides recognition for accomplishments. The self-paced, individualized approach demonstrates respect for each person's unique training needs and strengths. There are many opportunities for teachers to plan and make decisions about their learning. The greatest motivation, however, is to tie training and demonstration of competence to salary increases.

Applying the Principles of Adult Learning Theory

Adults bring a **wealth of previous experiences** to training. They find training more meaningful when their life experiences are recognized and they can relate the content to their own lives. For example, in each module the overview includes an opportunity for teachers to relate the content to their own lives and the pre-training assessment allows them to rate their own skills.

Adults need **opportunities to integrate new ideas with what they already know** so they can use the new information. Training should provide opportunities to make interpretations and draw conclusions. Many learning activities require teachers to answer questions about why they planned a specific activity, how children reacted, what they might do differently in the future, or how they can build on what they learned through the experience.

Adults **acquire conceptually new information more slowly** than information that relates to something they already know. The self-paced nature of this training program allows enough time for teachers to learn and apply new concepts. In addition, because some learning activities build on previous ones, new concepts are repeated and reinforced.

Adults tend to **acquire information even more slowly when it conflicts with what they already know**, because it forces them to re-evaluate their knowledge base. The trainer's feedback conferences with teachers can serve as opportunities to discuss and evaluate new knowledge.

Adults tend to **take errors personally** and some find it **difficult to take risks**. This training program encourages reflection, critical thinking, and skill development rather than focusing on "right" or "wrong" answers. Teachers are encouraged to use answer sheets as guides for learning, rather than view them as the only correct responses.

Adults **perceive their own experiences as unique and private**. They are not always comfortable or willing to share these experiences with others. Each teacher receives a copy of *Caring for Preschool Children,* which can serve as a personal journal of that individual's professional development. Trainers need to respect teachers' privacy while offering encouragement.

Research has shown that many adults learn best through a hands-on approach that actively involves them in the learning process. Edgar Dale explains this theory schematically in his "Cone of Experience," which follows.

Edgar Dale's Cone of Experience*

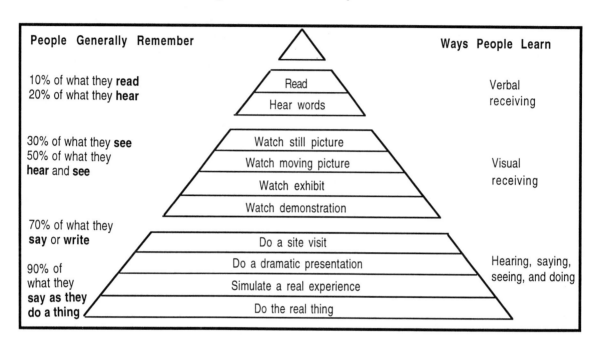

As noted earlier, the learning activities in *Caring for Preschool Children* are hands-on as they ask teachers to apply what they are learning. In addition to providing feedback after teachers have completed learning activities, trainers can plan their schedules to include time to observe teachers carrying out the activities.

* Based on Edgar Dale, *Audiovisual Methods in Teaching*; 3rd ed. (New York: Holt, Rinehart and Winston, 1969), p. 107.

Applying Adult Learning Principles to the Training

Principles of Adult Learning	What Trainers Can Do
Adults bring a wealth of experiences to training.	Use the overview and pre-training assessments to acknowledge what teachers already know.
Adults need time to integrate what they already know with new information.	Encourage teachers to reflect on their learning.
Adults need extra time to understand new information that doesn't relate to what they already know.	Respect the self-paced training approach so teachers can take as much time as they need to internalize new information.
Adults need even more time to integrate new information that conflicts with what they know.	Use feedback conferences to discuss and evaluate "new" and "old" knowledge.
Adults tend to take errors personally and some have difficulty taking risks.	Emphasize reflection and critical thinking rather than "right" or "wrong" answers.
Adults perceive their own experiences as unique and private.	Provide individual copies of training materials and respect each person's privacy while offering support and encouragement.
Adults learn best through a hands-on approach.	Observe teachers doing learning activities.

Chapter III

Overseeing the Training Program

Chapter III

Overseeing the Training Program

This chapter describes:

- Introducing the training program

- Completing the Orientation

- Completing a module

- Providing feedback

- Designing your own strategy for implementing a program

- Using the training materials in a mentoring program

- What teachers and trainers do to complete each module

Introducing the Training Program

When a program decides to implement *Caring for Preschool Children,* all teachers may not begin the training at the same time. Nevertheless, it is important for everyone to understand the value of the program and have a general understanding of the training content and process. You might hold a meeting to introduce the training program, explaining that it is part of the program's professional development and program improvement plans. Once the training program is fully implemented, you can meet with new teachers to provide an individualized overview of the training. A suggested agenda for either a group or individual introduction to *Caring for Preschool Children* follows.

A. Introduction

Use the Orientation in Volume I of *Caring for Preschool Children* and this *Trainer's Guide* to review the following topics and others specific to your situation.

- How the training meets the characteristics and circumstances of preschool teachers and programs.

- The content and organization of the training modules.

- The training approach—what teachers do and what the trainer does.

- Benefits to teachers, children, and families.

- The assessment process.

- Documentation of progress.

Display key points on overhead transparencies or chart paper and provide copies of *Caring for Preschool Children* so teachers can become familiar with its content and organization.

B. Discuss the Content and Training Approach

Ask teachers which topics and skills they would most like to learn about and in what order. Because *Caring for Preschool Children* is very comprehensive, you can demonstrate how these training requests are addressed in the modules.

Ask teachers to describe strategies that help them gain knowledge and skills. Teachers are likely to mention approaches such as observation and feedback by trainers, supervisors, or colleagues; viewing videotapes; reading books or articles; watching someone else perform a task; and discussing an idea or concept. Give specific examples that show how the *Caring for Preschool Children* training approach incorporates these strategies.

C. Provide an Overview of Observation and Recording

Explain that observation is a tool that teachers will use to complete many of the learning activities in this training program and throughout their early childhood professions. If appropriate, devote a block of time to review and practice the skills used to conduct and record systematic, objective, accurate and complete observations. You can use learning activity I, Using a Systematic Approach to Observing and Recording in Module 12, Program Management, as a resource.

Note that you will also conduct observations of teachers throughout the training program to learn more about each individual's involvement and interactions with children. You will use your observation notes as the basis for providing objective feedback to teachers on their progress in applying the knowledge and skills and to conduct the competency assessments.

D. Explain Your Plan for Conducting Feedback Conferences

Describe how the training program is tailored to each individual's needs, and also provides for a close working relationship between trainer and teacher. Emphasize that although teachers use use the materials independently, they are not left alone to sink or swim. Regular feedback is an integral part of the training process. Describe the purpose and frequency of feedback conferences and the approach (one-on-one, teaching teams, or group) you plan to use.

If you will be conducting group feedback meetings, explain that these are opportunities for teachers to discuss the learning activities and to support each other. Peer support can encourage teachers as they work with children each day and contribute to their professional growth.

E. Introduce the Individual Tracking Form

Distribute and review the individual tracking form found in Appendix C. Encourage teachers to monitor their own progress. Note that there is space for the trainer to sign off when each module is completed.

F. Describe the Plan for Acknowledging Teachers' Accomplishments

Emphasize that the program will acknowledge teachers for undertaking and completing the training program. Describe the program's plan for offering incentives such as the following.

- Award increases in salaries and benefits for successfully completing different levels of training.

- Give meaningful rewards for completing a substantial part of the training. For example, offer a certificate for dinner for two donated by a local restaurant, a new material for the children, or a copy of a favorite resource.

- Organize and display scrapbooks or picture albums that introduce the teachers to parents interested in enrolling their children in the program. Show pictures that highlight individual teachers interacting with children. Write brief summaries of teachers' special interests and accomplishments.

- Hold recognition dinners and award ceremonies for teachers who have completed the program. Invite spouses, parents, and other special guests.

- Offer child care so a teacher and guest can spend an evening out. Teachers might volunteer their child care services to acknowledge a colleague's success.

- Provide special pins, tote bags, or framed certificates that are concrete symbols of a teacher's completion of part or all of the program.

- Post on a bulletin board or include in the program newsletter photographs of teachers who have undertaken or completed the program.

G. Closing

Summarize the session and answer questions. Communicate your excitement about working with the teachers who are starting the training program. Describe the logistical arrangements for distributing materials, completing the Orientation, and scheduling individual meetings.

Completing the Orientation

The first step in the training program is completing the Orientation. Teachers read about the training program content and process and review the glossary and definitions of the CDA functional areas. Before they begin the first module, teachers complete the self-assessment. This exercise introduces the major topics and skills covered in each module and helps teachers select three modules with which they want to begin.

Encourage teachers to complete the self-assessment as honestly as possible. Honest answers will allow teachers to identify their strengths, interests, and needs.

Discuss with the Trainer: After completing the self-assessment, teachers meet with their trainer to review the Orientation and discuss their responses to the self-assessment. Allow enough time—15 to 30 minutes—at this meeting to identify the teacher's strengths, interests, and needs, and to work with the teacher to develop a module completion plan. The plan lists the first three modules a teacher plans to work on, with target completion dates, and a tentative schedule for completing the entire training program. It takes four to six weeks to complete all the learning activities in a module. The entire training program takes 12 to 18 months.

In general, the module completion plan is based on the responses to the self-assessment and the trainer's observation notes of the teacher working with children. In addition, the module completion plan might take into account program-wide improvement goals, such as reducing accidents and injuries or creating more effective learning environments. In such cases, teachers would all complete the same module so they can gain the knowledge and skills needed to achieve the program's goal.

The module completion plan is individualized for each teacher. However, in some cases, where a consultant is providing feedback and support, the plan will have to reflect the trainer's schedule as well. Many trainers find it helpful to encourage several teachers to work on the same module at the same time. This is especially useful when first implementing the training program or when training is tied to program improvement goals and strategies. Coordinating training plans in this way enables you to conduct group feedback sessions during which teachers can learn from and provide support to their colleagues. Also, group sessions make supervising the program less time-consuming for the trainer. But keep in mind that some teachers may benefit from individualized feedback on modules in which their skills are less developed.

Completing a Module

Although the content and activities in the modules vary substantially, teachers and trainers follow the same process for completing each one. The process for completing each section of a module is described below and illustrated in the diagram on page 31.

Overview

Teachers read about the topics and three major skills addressed in the module. For each skill, they review concrete examples depicting teachers demonstrating their competence and a short situation illustrating teachers applying their skills. Teachers answer questions about each situation and compare their answers to those on the answer sheets at the end of the module. Next, teachers answer questions about how the topic relates to their own experiences, both on and off the job.

As each teacher begins the training program, try to schedule a one-hour observation of the individual working with children. If teachers seem uncomfortable with being observed, begin by conducting brief observations and immediately holding a feedback conference to share what you saw and heard. As teachers recognize the value of having an observer take objective notes on what takes place in the program, they are likely to become more comfortable with your presence and you can increase the length of the observation period.

Pre-Training Assessment

Teachers complete the pre-training assessment—a list of the skills described in the concrete examples depicting teachers demonstrating their competence—by indicating whether they do these things regularly, sometimes, or not enough. They review their responses and identify three to five skills they want to improve or topics they want to know learn more about. Teachers can refer to the glossary at the end of the module if they need definitions for the terms used.

Discuss with the Trainer: Teachers then meet with you to discuss their responses to the Overview and pre-training assessment. They then begin the learning activities for the module.

Learning Activities

Each module contains five to six learning activities. Teachers read several pages of information about the topic. Next, they apply their knowledge while working with children and families. For example, they might answer questions related to the reading and their own teaching practices; complete a checklist; try out suggestions from the reading and report on the results; plan, implement, and evaluate an activity; or observe and record children's behavior and interactions, then use the observation notes to individualize the program. Examples of completed forms, summaries, and charts are provided, when needed, to demonstrate how to do the activity.

Trainers offer ongoing support to teachers as they complete the learning activities. Support might include observations of the teacher implementing an activity, conducting a co-observation of a child, reviewing plans and assisting in collecting materials, or discussing and answering questions about the content.

Discuss with the Trainer: Teachers meet with the trainer after completing most learning activities. They discuss the content and report on what they did and what they learned. Trainers provide feedback based on observation notes and on the written portion of the learning activity—charts, checklists, plans, responses to questions, or observation summaries. For some activities, teachers meet with colleagues or a child's parents, or review answer sheets at the end of the module.

Summarizing Your Progress

After completing all of the learning activities, teachers take time to summarize their progress. They review their responses to the pre-training assessment and describe their increased knowledge and skills. For some modules, teachers also review and add to one of the learning activities.

Discuss with the Trainer: Teachers meet with their trainer to review their progress and to discuss whether they are ready for the knowledge and competency assessments. If teachers are ready for assessment, you can schedule a time to administer the knowledge assessment and conduct the competency assessment observation. If teachers need further training on the topics and skills addressed in the module, you can help them plan strategies for continuing to develop the necessary knowledge and skills.

For teachers who are having difficulty mastering the skills and knowledge in a module, or for those who want to learn more about a specific topic you might suggest other resources. Professional organizations and publishers offer numerous books, journals, videotapes, and training manuals related to caring for preschool children. The Orientation in Volume I of *Caring for Preschool Children* includes an extensive bibliography of resources for early childhood professionals.

Assessing Competence

There is a knowledge assessment for each module and a competency assessment for Modules 1 through 12. Chapter V of this *Trainer's Guide*, Assessing Each Teacher's Progress, describes the assessment process, offers guidance on administering, scoring, and discussing the results, and includes the knowledge assessments and competency assessment observation forms.

Documenting Progress

After teachers have successfully completed the learning activities and both assessments, they can record their progress on the Individual Tracking Form (included in Appendix C) and ask for the trainer's sign-off. Trainers use the Program Tracking Form (also in Appendix C) to document and monitor progress of a group of teachers who are working on the modules. Keeping this form up to date can help you schedule feedback sessions and assessments. The diagram on the next page illustrates the training process.

Providing Feedback

Whether provided one-on-one or during group sessions, the trainer's feedback to teachers is crucial to the success of *Caring for Preschool Children*. Feedback conferences are particularly important because of the self-instructional nature of the training program. These conferences give trainers regular contact with teachers. They are opportunities for trainers to answer questions, offer support, make suggestions, listen to concerns about progress, reinforce new skills, help teachers recognize how much they have learned, and encourage teachers to repeat activities they may have misunderstood the first time.

For each module, trainers provide feedback after teachers complete:

- the overview and pre-training assessment;

- most learning activities;

- the summarizing your progress section; and

- the knowledge and competency assessments.

Feedback conferences may be as short as 10 minutes or may last longer, depending on how much feedback and support teachers need. Try to schedule feedback conferences for the learning activities before teachers begin the next ones. To make sure teachers have understood the content, it is always best to discuss responses that are still fresh in their minds. A full understanding of each activity is particularly important when the next learning activity builds on the knowledge and skills addressed in the previous one.

Encourage teachers to take the initiative in scheduling feedback conferences. You can post a schedule of times when you are free and encourage teachers to sign up when ready. When several teachers are working on the same module, the decision on when to meet should be a joint one, because everyone will have to be at the same point in the module at the time of the feedback conference.

Here are some suggestions for conducting one-on-one or group feedback sessions. You can adapt them to reflect your own training style and what you know about each teacher.

- **Review the written responses in each learning activity before the conference.** This is especially important when preparing to give feedback on inappropriate responses. Consider how to offer constructive comments that encourage teachers to try an activity again.

- **Begin with an open-ended question.** For example, "How did you feel about this activity?" or "What did you learn from this activity?" Take a few minutes to discuss each teacher's responses to the questions.

The Training Process

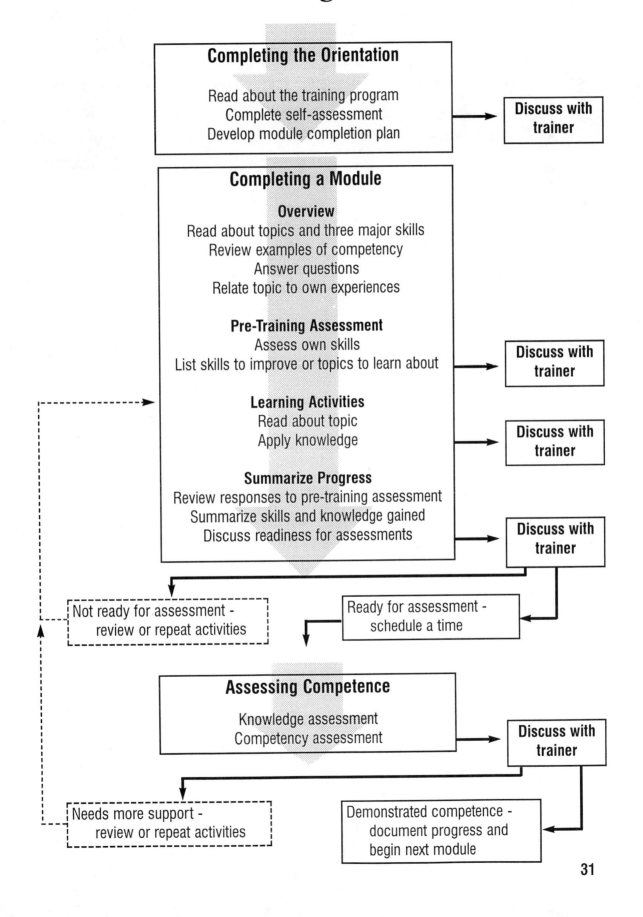

Completing the Orientation

Read about the training program
Complete self-assessment
Develop module completion plan

→ **Discuss with trainer**

Completing a Module

Overview
Read about topics and three major skills
Review examples of competency
Answer questions
Relate topic to own experiences

Pre-Training Assessment
Assess own skills
List skills to improve or topics to learn about

→ **Discuss with trainer**

Learning Activities
Read about topic
Apply knowledge

→ **Discuss with trainer**

Summarize Progress
Review responses to pre-training assessment
Summarize skills and knowledge gained
Discuss readiness for assessments

→ **Discuss with trainer**

Not ready for assessment - review or repeat activities

Ready for assessment - schedule a time

Assessing Competence

Knowledge assessment
Competency assessment

→ **Discuss with trainer**

Needs more support - review or repeat activities

Demonstrated competence - document progress and begin next module

- **Use specific examples to acknowledge appropriate responses.** For example: "The way you phrased that showed your respect for Karl. You told him clearly what you expected, but you were careful to show him you understood his feelings."

- **Relate teachers' responses to information in the text.** For example: "Your responses show that you understand how to use the suggested strategies for handling challenging behaviors and why they are appropriate."

- **Ask questions about inappropriate responses.** Instead of simply correcting them, help the teacher think about why a response is inappropriate and what effect it might have on a child. For example:

  "What do you think are the reasons for LaShonda's behavior?"

  "How could you involve the children in this routine?"

  "What message would this statement give to the child?"

- **Help teachers arrive at more appropriate responses.** You might say:

  "Let's look back at the text. Perhaps there's another way to phrase this so it offers guidance without making the child feel discouraged."

The underlying goal of providing feedback is to improve a teacher's skills and knowledge. If a teacher has not understood the information presented in a learning activity, use the feedback conference to review and explain the information and promote understanding. Specific strategies for extending learning are provided at the end of this chapter.

Designing Your Own Strategy for Implementing the Training

This chapter has described one approach to implementing *Caring for Preschool Children*. Many programs choose to tailor this approach so that it fits the needs and circumstances of their teachers and trainers. The training materials to be flexible enough are used to meet a variety of goals. Here are some examples:

- **Observation Training:** At the start of each year, all teachers attend a workshop on observation skills which is based on the learning activities in Module 12, Program Management. This is an opportunity for experienced teachers to brush up on observation and for new teachers to develop this important skill. Throughout the year teachers use observation skills to complete learning activities and as a regular part of their work.

- **Orientation Training:** When new teachers are hired by the program they complete the overview sections of selected modules to help them to begin gaining the knowledge and skills needed to care for preschool children. Later, new teachers go back and complete the Orientation in Volume I, develop individual module completion plans, and begin working on the modules.

- **Program Improvement Efforts:** After reviewing the results of a comprehensive program assessment, the trainer and teachers focus on those modules that are directly tied to identified weaknesses. For example, all teachers work on the Families module because the assessment showed that the program was not offering a variety of parent involvement options.

When designing a strategy for tailoring the training materials to address program needs, it helps to develop a training plan. Your plan should address the principles of adult learning and answer the following questions:

- What are the goals for the training? What specific needs will it meet?

- What skills and knowledge will be addressed?

- Where will the training take place?

- Who will participate in the training? How many teachers will take part? What are their levels of experience and knowledge?

- Who will serve as the trainer?

- How will the trainer provide ongoing support to participants?

- How will the trainer conduct regular observations of participants while they are working with children and share his or her observation notes?

- How will the trainer review and give participants feedback on their completed learning activities?

- How will the trainer administer and discuss the assessments?

Developing a training plan ensures that you will include the key features described in Chapter II: individualizing, providing ongoing feedback based on regular, systematic observations, incorporating hands-on learning, and assessing knowledge and competence.

Using the Training Materials in a Mentoring Program

Mentor teachers are experienced early childhood educators who give individualized support to teachers new to the profession. Generally, mentor teachers have sufficient teaching experience to be recognized for their expertise. They have knowledge of child development and developmentally appropriate practices and are skilled in planning for and interacting with children. Effective mentor teachers are skilled observers and effective communicators. They regularly reflect on their own behaviors and recognize the importance of being life-long learners. They guide teachers through the planning process, help them develop specific skills, and model appropriate practice.

Two features are critical to the success of mentoring programs. First, there should be a mechanism for mentors to get support from each other or a supervisor. Mentors need to discuss their experiences and teachers' reactions, problem solve, and share successes. In addition, it is important to include opportunities for teachers to give feedback to mentors during their regularly scheduled meetings and at periodic intervals, perhaps during meetings between the mentor teacher, teacher, and supervisor.

Mentor teachers can use *Caring for Preschool Children* as the framework and content for an organized mentoring program. While overseeing the training, mentor teachers can meet with teachers at regular, scheduled times; observe teachers working with children and families; model appropriate practices; review completed learning activities; give written and verbal feedback; answer teachers' questions; provide ongoing support; and administer and discuss assessments. While supporting the training process, mentor teachers can also serve as a key source of support for new teachers. Mentor teachers can answer questions and respond to new teachers' concerns, whether related to the training or other job-related issues. When new teachers receive ongoing support, they are more likely to remain on the job and become committed to long-term professional growth and development.

What Teachers and Trainers Do in Each Module

The following charts summarize what the teachers and trainers do in each section of the 13 modules. Individual teachers and trainers have different learning and interaction styles. Thus, these charts do not present hard-and-fast rules to be followed inflexibly. Rather, they summarize what teachers are asked to do and suggest constructive ways trainers can provide support. Each chart is followed by suggested strategies for extending learning in individual or group sessions.

Completing Module 1: Safe

Learning Activity	What Teachers Do	What Trainers Do

Overview and Pre-Training Assessment	Read about safety and what teachers can do to keep children safe.
	
	Read examples of teachers keeping children safe and answer questions.
	
	Answer questions about a personal safety experience.
	
	Complete pre-training assessment and list three to five skills to improve or topics to learn more about.
	
	Discuss overview and pre-training assessment with the trainer.
		Review their ongoing written observations of teachers.
		
		Discuss with teachers:
		
		   responses to questions;
		
		   personal safety experience and how this relates to keeping children safe; and
		
		   pre-training assessment.
		
		Validate pre-training assessment where possible with their written observations.

I. Using Your Knowledge of Child Development to Keep Children Safe	Read about ways teachers can promote safety while encouraging children's risk-taking behavior. Complete chart showing how teachers can use child development information to keep children safe. Discuss chart with the trainer. Continue adding to the chart while working on the module.	Discuss what teachers can do to help children take risks safely. Discuss examples listed on charts. Share their observations of instances teachers ensured children's safety. Encourage teachers to add to chart while working on the module.
II. Creating and Maintaining a Safe Environment	Read about safety precautions and ways to create and maintain safe indoor and outdoor environments. Use indoor and outdoor checklists to assess safety conditions. List unsafe items and steps needed to improve safety. Discuss suggested improvements with colleagues and the trainer. Make and check off changes. With colleagues, develop a schedule for daily and monthly safety checks.	Review checklists and potential dangers identified. Help teachers plan ways to make the needed changes. Check back to ensure teachers made changes to improve safety conditions in the environment.

Module 1: Safe (continued)

Learning Activity	What Teachers Do	What Trainers Do
III. Handling Accidents and Emergencies	Read about responding to injuries, first aid procedures, and handling fires and other emergencies. Review program emergency and accident procedures and answer questions about how to respond to accidents and emergencies. Discuss answers with the trainer. If needed, review program's emergency procedures with supervisor.	Discuss answers to questions. Encourage teachers to review and practice emergency procedures on a regular basis. Provide additional resources and training on responding to accidents and emergencies, as needed.
IV. Ensuring Children's Safety Away from the Program	Read about safe practices for walks and field trips. Answer questions about program policies and procedures for walks and field trips. List safety precautions to add to those already used by program. Discuss answers with colleagues and the trainer.	Discuss answers to questions. Encourage teachers to use simple, positive language when discussing ways to take safety precautions.
V. Helping Children Learn to Keep Themselves Safe	Read about helping children learn to keep themselves safe by modeling, explaining safety practices, and involving children in developing safety rules. Work with a small group of children to develop safety limits for an indoor and outdoor interest area. Answer questions about the process. Discuss responses with colleagues and the trainer.	Help teachers plan a safety discussion with children, if asked. If possible, observe teachers conducting the activity and provide feedback. Discuss responses to the questions.
Summarizing Your Progress	Review and add examples to charts from Learning Activity I. Review responses to pre-training assessment, summarize what was learned in this module, and list skills developed or improved.	Discuss summary of progress. Schedule assessments for this module.

Module 1: Safe (continued)

Strategies for Extending Learning

- Have teachers kneel on the floor to view the environment from the children's perspective. Discuss any potential hazards teachers discovered.

- Distribute information on and encourage teachers to attend safety training courses or workshops offered at the program, by local hospitals, or by national groups such as the Red Cross.

- Ask teachers to individualize the safety checklists to reflect their room arrangement, furnishings, materials, equipment, and outdoor areas.

- Encourage teachers to keep records of how they address potentially dangerous items and conditions they identify. This exercise will help teachers develop an awareness that maintaining a safe environment is an ongoing part of their jobs.

- Suggest that teachers obtain and share with parents safety publications from organizations such as the American Academy of Pediatrics and the Consumer Product Safety Commission.

- Ask the local Red Cross or fire department to provide training on how to respond during weather-related emergencies such as lightning storms, tornadoes, and earthquakes.

- Make a scrapbook highlighting teachers' actions that kept children safe in an emergency or crisis.

- Have teachers work with children to develop and post safety limits for each indoor and outdoor interest area.

Completing Module 2: Healthy

Learning Activity	What Teachers Do	What Trainers Do
Overview and Pre-Training Assessment	Read about health, hygiene, nutrition, and child abuse and neglect and what teachers can do to keep children healthy. Read examples of situations in which teachers ensured children's health and answer questions. Answer questions about personal health and nutrition habits. Complete pre-training assessment and list three to five skills to improve or topics to learn more about. Discuss overview and pre-training assessment with the trainer.	Review their ongoing written observations of teachers. Discuss with teachers: responses to questions; personal health habits (if teachers wish to share them) and how they relate to keeping children healthy; and pre-training assessment. Validate pre-training assessment where possible with their written observations.
I. Maintaining a Hygienic Environment	Read about sanitary procedures such as using bleach solutions that reduce illness. Use a health and hygiene checklist to assess routines. List items that need improvement and improvement strategies. Discuss strategies with colleagues and the trainer. Make and check off needed changes.	Review completed checklists as well as items that need improvement. Meet with teachers and colleagues to discuss improvement strategies that will make the environment more hygienic. Suggest other items that might need improvement.
II. Responding When Children Are Sick	Read about daily health checks, signs of illnesses, symptoms of contagious diseases, administering medication, HIV, and lice. Review program's policies on sick children and contagious illnesses. Apply the policies in response to vignettes. Discuss the activity with the trainer.	Review responses to vignettes. Answer questions and discuss concerns about the transmission of contagious illnesses. Help teachers learn more about HIV and other illnesses and conditions that affect young children.

Module 2: Healthy (continued)

Learning Activity	What Teachers Do	What Trainers Do
III. Encouraging Good Nutrition	Read about the United States Department of Agriculture Child and Adult Care Food Program (USDA/CACFP), family-style meals, and cooking with children. Plan, conduct, and report on a small group cooking activity. Discuss the cooking activity with the children's parents and the trainer. Offer parents suggestions for cooking with children at home.	Offer to help collect resources and ingredients for the cooking activity. If possible, observe teachers conducting the activity. Discuss activity summary. Help teachers plan ways to involve children in preparing and serving meals and snacks.
IV. Helping Children Learn Healthy Habits	Read about teaching children good health habits through routines, play, and activities. Describe a routine usually done without children. Plan and implement a strategy for including children in the routine. Report on what happened. Discuss the activity with colleagues and the trainer. If appropriate, change the routine permanently.	Discuss with teachers how they changed their approach in carrying out one routine. Focus on the healthy habits children learn by actively participating in routines. Help teachers examine and make necessary changes to other routines so that children are involved as much as possible.
V. Recognizing the Signs of Possible Child Abuse and Neglect	Read the definitions and signs of different types of abuse and neglect. Also, read about picking up clues from families and the signs of child abuse or neglect in child care settings. Answer questions about child abuse and neglect. Review the answer sheet at the end of the module. Discuss the activity with the trainer.	Review the different types and signs of child abuse and neglect. Provide definitions and guidance on child abuse and neglect information from the program, and state and local jurisdictions. Review answers to the questions and compare to those provided at the end of the module.

Module 2: Healthy (continued)

Learning Activity	What Teachers Do	What Trainers Do
VI. Reporting Suspected Cases of Child Abuse and Neglect	Read about state and local laws and policies for reporting child abuse and neglect. Use program's child abuse and neglect reporting procedures to complete chart listing key information. Read about overcoming barriers to reporting, getting ready to report, and what to do after a report is filed. Review a checklist for reporters. Answer questions about teachers' responsibilities for reporting suspected child abuse and neglect. Review the answer sheet at the end of the module. Discuss the activity with the trainer.	If needed, provide a copy of the program's policy and procedures for reporting child abuse and neglect. Emphasize that it is a teachers' responsibility to report suspected child abuse and neglect, and that they do not have to provide proof. Review answers to the questions and compare to those provided at the end of the module. Answer additional questions and help alleviate remaining concerns regarding reporting suspected child abuse and neglect.
Summarizing Your Progress	Review responses to pre-training assessment, summarize what was learned in this module, and list skills developed or improved.	Discuss summary of progress. Schedule assessments for this module.

Strategies for Extending Learning

- Ask teachers to review and discuss the program's menus for snacks and meals. Recommend changes, if necessary, to ensure foods served to children meet USDA/CACFP guidelines.

- Suggest that teachers ask parents to share their favorite recipes from home. Provide materials so teachers can turn these into picture recipe cards.

- Maintain and share with teachers a file of recipes and plans for simple cooking activities. Encourage teachers to maintain their own files. Suggest that they take photographs of children during cooking activities and share with parents and colleagues.

- Serve healthy snacks at staff meetings and workshops. Discuss ways teachers can model good nutrition and hygiene practices, such as healthy eating habits and washing their hands before eating.

- Ask teachers to help you organize a collection of resources on the prevention of child abuse and neglect. Work together to plan and implement family support activities at the program.

- Visit a program at meal or snack time so you can model strategies for relaxed, family-style dining—before, during, and after eating.

- Encourage teachers to meet regularly to discuss stresses that may be affecting children and families and to suggest strategies for offering assistance. Ask teachers to share their healthy approaches to dealing with stress, and encourage them to support each other on the job.

Completing Module 3: Learning Environment

Learning Activity	What Teachers Do	What Trainers Do
Overview and Pre-Training Assessment	Read about what teachers can do to create and use effective indoor and outdoor learning environments. Read examples of situations in which teachers created and used learning environments for preschool children and answer questions. Answer questions about the effects of being in different kinds of environments. Complete pre-training assessment and list three to five skills to improve or topics to learn more about. Discuss overview and pre-training assessment with the trainer.	Review their ongoing written observations of teachers and learning environments. Discuss with teachers: responses to questions; personal experiences in different environments and how this relates to creating appropriate learning environments; and pre-training assessment. Validate pre-training assessment where possible with their written observations.
I. Using Your Knowledge of Child Development to Create a Learning Environment	Read about how preschool children actively explore the environment. Complete chart showing how teachers can use child development information to create a learning environment. Discuss chart with the trainer. Continue adding to the chart while working on the module.	Discuss what teachers can do to create environments that reflect and support children's development. Discuss examples recorded on charts. Share their observations of children using the learning environment. Encourage teachers to add to the chart while working on the module.
II. Conveying Positive Messages Through the Environment	Read about sending children positive messages through the environment. Complete chart describing how the environment conveys different messages and listing new ideas to try. Discuss ideas with colleagues, agree on changes to try, make changes, and record children's reactions. Discuss the activity with the trainer.	Review teachers' ideas and guide them to add others, if appropriate. Offer to help teachers get materials needed to make changes. Discuss how children reacted to changes.

Module 3: Learning Environment (continued)

Learning Activity	What Teachers Do	What Trainers Do
III. Establishing Interest Areas in the Classroom	Read about interest areas for preschool children. Identify and compare the strengths and weaknesses of two classroom arrangements. Draw their classroom floor plan. Draw a second plan with changes and additions based on the module. Discuss revised floor plans with colleagues and agree on changes. Record children's reactions to changes. Discuss the activity with the trainer.	Compare the strengths and weaknesses of each floor plan. Discuss plans to improve the environment. If possible, meet with teachers and their colleagues to review proposed changes and encourage teamwork. Help teachers rearrange the environment according to their plans. Encourage teachers to observe children regularly for reactions to the environment and to determine when additional changes are needed.
IV. Selecting and Displaying Materials	Read about how to select, organize and display appropriate materials. Use a checklist to identify items in nine indoor interest areas and assess how materials are organized and displayed. List materials to add to interest areas. Review checklist with colleagues and the trainer and decide on changes. Note children's reactions.	Review completed checklists and recommended additions. Discuss how new items will enhance children's development and how they will be organized and displayed. If appropriate, help teachers obtain or make new items. Encourage teachers to propose new purchases to their supervisors.
V. Organizing the Outdoor Environment	Read about the characteristics of outdoor environments that offer children a range of experiences. Review a chart of materials and equipment for outdoor activities and ways children use them. Identify current outdoor activities. Develop and implement plans to add or improve three activities. Report on what children do. Discuss the activity with the trainer.	Review and discuss plans. Ask teachers to explain how the plans will give children new experiences. If appropriate, help teachers obtain or make new items. Discuss children's reactions to the changes.

Module 3: Learning Environment (continued)

Learning Activity	What Teachers Do	What Trainers Do
VI. Planning the Daily Schedule, Routines, and Transitions	Read about appropriate daily schedules, routines, and transitions. Review a sample schedule and describe why it is appropriate for preschool children. Assess the daily schedule and decide on needed changes. Discuss the activity with colleagues and the trainer.	Discuss the effectiveness of daily schedules and plans for carrying out routines. Have teachers determine what changes are needed. If possible, observe routines and transitions. Help teachers identify problems and propose solutions.
Summarizing Your Progress	Review and add examples to charts from Learning Activity I. Review responses to pre-training assessment, summarize what was learned in this module, and list skills developed or improved.	Discuss summary of progress. Schedule assessments for this module.

Strategies for Extending Learning

- Show the slide/video *The NEW Room Arrangement as a Teaching Strategy* and discuss ideas teachers would like to try to make their indoor learning environments more appropriate for and responsive to the children in their care.

- Collect materials for making classroom labels (e.g., clear and solid colors of adhesive paper, poster board, construction paper, permanent markers, glue).

- Suggest that teachers plan and hold a workshop for parents on learning environments at the center and at home. Discuss topics such as:

  - messages in the environment;
  - how the environment promotes active learning; and
  - how children learn to take care of the environment.

- Hold a workshop on adapting indoor and outdoor environments for children with special needs. Cover the relevant requirements of the 1990 Americans with Disabilities Act (ADA) and offer specific strategies that respond to the needs of children enrolled. Contact the Educational Resources Information Center (ERIC) Clearinghouse on Disabilities and Gifted Children (1-800-328-0272) for information and suggested resources.

- Help teachers set up a system for collecting and storing "found" materials (e.g., dramatic play props, cardboard boxes, plastic containers, paper, fabric scraps).

Completing Module 4: Physical

Learning Activity	What Teachers Do	What Trainers Do
Overview and Pre-Training Assessment	Read about gross and fine motor development, the link between physical fitness and self-esteem, and what teachers can do to promote preschool children's physical development. Read examples of situations in which teachers promoted physical development and answer questions. Answer questions about staying physically fit by maintaining good posture and flexibility. Complete pre-training assessment and list three to five skills to improve or topics to learn more about. Discuss overview and pre-training assessment with the trainer.	Review their ongoing written observations of teachers. Discuss with teachers: responses to questions; plans to improve posture and movements; and pre-training assessment. Validate pre-training assessment where possible with their written observations.
I. Using Your Knowledge of Child Development to Promote Gross Motor Skills	Read about preschool children's development of gross motor skills. Complete chart showing how teachers can use child development information to promote children's gross motor skills. Discuss chart with the trainer. Continue adding to the chart while working on the module.	Discuss what teachers can do to encourage children to develop and use gross motor skills. Review examples recorded on charts. Share their observations of children using gross motor skills. Encourage teachers to add to the chart while working on the module.
II. Observing and Planning for Children's Fine Motor Development	Read about how preschool children develop fine motor skills and use senses to coordinate movement. Observe two children using fine motor skills. Summarize each child's fine motor skills and challenges and list ways to promote fine motor development. Discuss the activity with colleagues and the trainer.	Discuss observation summaries. Suggest materials, routines, and activities that will give children opportunities to develop and practice fine motor skills.

Module 4: Physical (continued)

Learning Activity	What Teachers Do	What Trainers Do
III. Encouraging Physical Fitness	Read about how teachers can help children learn gross motor skills, how outdoor play promotes physical fitness, and how to provide indoor physical activities. Plan and implement an open-ended fitness activity. Report on what happened and describe plans for repeating or changing the activity. Discuss with parents of children who participated and the trainer. Encourage parents to include children in family fitness activities.	Review activity plans and summaries and discuss how the activity encouraged children's physical fitness. Suggest other open-ended activities that appeal to groups of children with a wide range of interests and physical abilities. Offer to review indoor and outdoor environments to make sure children have daily opportunities to use their large muscles and stay physically fit.
IV. Creating an Environment That Supports Physical Development	Read about the importance of creating an environment that allows children of varied skill levels to use their fine and gross motor skills. Review a chart describing typical opportunities for using fine and gross motor skills in each interest area. Add their ideas to the chart. Observe one child working on a fine motor skill and one child working on a gross motor skill. For each skill, suggest appropriate materials to promote development. Discuss the activity with colleagues and the trainer.	Discuss ideas listed on charts. If appropriate, suggest materials and activities. Review and discuss observation summaries. Ask teachers to explain how the suggested materials promote use of the fine or gross motor skill. Suggest completing this activity for other children.
V. Promoting Positive Self-Concepts Through Development of Physical Skills	Read about the relationship between physical development and positive self-concepts and how teachers' interactions with children can encourage a sense of competence. Read examples of children using physical skills, list appropriate activities and materials, and suggest what to say to encourage the child. Discuss the responses with the trainer.	Review and discuss responses, offer feedback, and give suggestions if needed. Discuss ways to help individual children feel successful, regardless of the level of their physical skills.

Module 4: Physical (continued)

Learning Activity	What Teachers Do	What Trainers Do
Summarizing Your Progress	Review and add examples to charts from Learning Activity I. Review responses to pre-training assessment, summarize what was learned in this module, and list skills developed or improved.	Discuss summary of progress. Schedule assessments for this module.

Strategies for Extending Learning

- Observe children about whom teachers are concerned—children who seem to have unusual delays in fine or gross motor skill development. Share your observation notes with teachers and, if needed, with the children's parents. Encourage parents to follow up with their pediatrician or a specialist, if necessary.

- Hold a workshop in which teachers use their fine motor skills as children do during activities such as woodworking, fingerpainting, cooking, doing puzzles, setting the table, building with Legos, stringing beads, water play, and outdoor mural painting. Point out the small muscle skills developed through these and similar activities.

- Lead role plays so teachers can practice encouraging children who are developing physical skills. Ask two teachers to pretend they are children engaged in an activity while a third teacher provides encouragement. Switch roles so everyone has a turn playing each role. Discuss how it feels to give and receive encouragement.

- Ask teachers to assume responsibility for teaching their colleagues how to play a non-competitive game or conduct an activity that encourages physical fitness. Provide blank forms so teachers can describe the game or activity, list the materials and equipment, present guidelines, and suggest variations so children with a wide range of physical skills can join in.

Completing Module 5: Cognitive

Learning Activity	What Teachers Do	What Trainers Do
Overview and Pre-Training Assessment	Read about theories of cognitive development and what teachers can do to promote preschool children's thinking skills. Read examples of situations in which teachers guided children's cognitive development and answer questions. Read about learning styles and factors that affect the ability to learn. List factors that have helped them become successful learners. Complete pre-training assessment and list three to five skills to improve or topics to learn more about. Discuss overview and pre-training assessment with the trainer.	Review their ongoing written observations of teachers. Discuss with teachers: responses to questions; individual learning styles and how this relates to helping children become lifelong learners; and pre-training assessment. Validate pre-training assessment where possible with their written observations.
I. Using Your Knowledge of Child Development to Promote Cognitive Development	Read about the way preschool children construct knowledge about the world. Complete chart showing how teachers can use child development information to promote children's cognitive development. Discuss chart with the trainer. Continue adding to the chart while working on the module.	Discuss what teachers can do to encourage children's cognitive development. Review examples recorded on charts. Share their observations of children using thinking and problem-solving skills. Encourage teachers to add to the chart while working on the module.
II. Understanding How Preschool Children Think	Read about the characteristics of preschool children's thinking as they attempt to make sense of the world. Over a one-week period, observe and record examples of children using thinking skills to make sense of the world. Discuss the activity with the trainer.	Discuss observations of children making sense of the world. If possible, conduct joint observations. Share notes with teachers and discuss how children expand their thinking.

Module 5: Cognitive (continued)

Learning Activity	What Teachers Do	What Trainers Do
III. Encouraging Children to Explore and Discover	Read about how children use a variety of skills to explore the world and make discoveries and how asking open-ended questions helps children build on what they already know. Observe and note examples of children using thinking skills as they work and play indoors and outdoors. Record what the children did and what teachers said to promote learning and thinking. Discuss the activity with the trainer.	Discuss observation summaries and how open-ended questions promoted thinking and learning. Discuss ways to make sure the environment, activities, routines, and teacher interactions offer opportunities for children to: notice characteristics; identify similarities and differences; classify; sequence; and observe cause and effect.
IV. Planning Experiences with Sand and Water	Read about how children construct knowledge, use props, and engage in planned experiences through sand and water play. Plan, implement, and describe what happens during a sand and water activity. Discuss the activity with the trainer.	Discuss sand and water play activity plans. Ask teachers to describe what children did that differed from what they had expected. If appropriate, help teachers establish a system for collecting and sharing sand and water play props.
V. Helping Children Develop Problem-Solving Skills	Read about the importance of: letting children solve their own problems; creating an environment that encourages problem solving; and involving children in resolving classroom problems. Identify a problem. Discuss it with children and involve them in finding a solution. Report on what happens. Discuss the activity with the trainer.	If possible, observe teachers leading children in the problem-solving exercise. Discuss what happened and how children were actively involved in developing and implementing solutions. Discuss how teachers can encourage children to be problem-solvers rather than stepping in to solve problems for them.

Module 5: Cognitive (continued)

Learning Activity	What Teachers Do	What Trainers Do
VI. Engaging Children in Long-Term Studies	Read about appropriate topics for long-term studies and the value of offering materials and experiences that enable children to recreate what they are learning. Develop a plan for a long-term study that responds to children's immediate interests. Discuss the plan with colleagues and the trainer.	Discuss long-term study plans. Suggest additional materials, resources, and experiences, if appropriate. Offer to help teachers implement their plans. Spend time during regular observations focusing on what's happening with the long-term study. Remind teachers to observe children engaged in the long-term study so they will know what materials and experiences to offer in response to children's changing skills and interests.
Summarizing Your Progress	Review and add examples to charts from Learning Activity I. Review responses to pre-training assessment, summarize what was learned in this module, and list skills developed or improved.	Discuss summary of progress. Schedule assessments for this module.

Strategies for Extending Learning

- During visits to programs, model ways of asking open-ended questions that encourage children to expand their thinking.

- Suggest that teachers establish a schedule for regularly assessing how well the materials in interest areas promote children's cognitive skills. Teachers can replace items that are either too challenging or not challenging enough.

- Have teachers collect examples of children's statements and conversations that demonstrate use of thinking skills. Use the examples to begin a discussion of how children make sense of the world.

- Identify possible appropriate topics for long-term studies (a construction project near the program, a ship docking in the harbor). Work with teachers to plan ways to expose children to these events to see whether they are interested in learning more about them.

Completing Module 6: Communication

Learning Activity	What Teachers Do	What Trainers Do
Overview and Pre-Training Assessment	Read about communication and language skills and what teachers can do to promote children's communication skills. Read examples of situations in which teachers promoted children's communication skills and answer questions. Read and complete a checklist about personal communication skills. Complete pre-training assessment and list three to five skills to improve or topics to learn more about. Discuss overview and pre-training assessment with the trainer.	Review their ongoing written observations of teachers. Discuss with teachers: responses to questions; self-assessment of communication skills and how this relates to promoting children's communication skills; and pre-training assessment. Validate pre-training assessment where possible with their written observations.
I. Using Your Knowledge of Child Development to Promote Language Skills	Read about how preschool children learn to use language and how teachers can promote communication skills. Complete chart showing how teachers can use child development information to promote children's communication skills. Discuss chart with the trainer. Continue adding to the chart while working on the module.	Discuss what teachers can do to help children develop and use communication skills. Review examples recorded on charts. Share their observations of children using language in different ways. Encourage teachers to add to the chart while working on the module.
II. Observing Children's Listening and Speaking Skills	Read about how preschool children learn to listen and speak. Read also about signs of possible speech or language disorders. Observe the language skills of two children during a one-week period. Complete summaries of each child's listening and talking skills. Discuss the activity with the trainer.	If possible, observe the same two children using listening and talking skills. Discuss the completed summaries. Explain that teachers will use the observation summaries in the next activity.

Module 6: Communication (continued)

Learning Activity	What Teachers Do	What Trainers Do
III. Encouraging Children to Listen and Speak	Read about creating an environment that supports communication and how teachers can help children learn the rules of conversation and expand their understanding and vocabularies. Use observation notes of the two children from the previous activity to plan strategies and activities to encourage their listening and speaking. Try strategies and activities for two weeks and report on results. Discuss the activity with the trainer.	Review observation summaries from previous activity and the plan for using specific strategies and activities to encourage listening and speaking. Offer feedback and suggestions. Discuss what happened during the two-week period and how teachers can continue encouraging all children to listen and speak.
IV. Reading Books with Preschool Children	Read about: selecting books to match children's skills, interests, and characteristics; setting up a library area; reading to individual children and to small groups; and extending children's enjoyment of books. Select two books that are appropriate for the children in the classroom. Read one to a small group and one to an individual child. Report on each experience. Discuss the activity with the trainer.	Encourage teachers to assess their book inventories regularly to make sure the current selections reflect and build on children's skills, interests, experiences, and characteristics. Discuss reports on reading to small groups and individuals. Compare the two experiences. Suggest teachers keep track of times they read to individuals to make sure every child has regular one-on-one reading experiences.
V. Supporting Emerging Literacy Skills	Read about emerging literacy; the stages children pass through as they learn to read and write; and how to create a print-rich environment. Observe, describe, and plan ways to support a child's emerging literacy. List ways the indoor environment encourages emerging literacy. Try five new ways to support emerging literacy and report on the results. Discuss the activity with the trainer.	Review and discuss how children explore and gradually gain literacy skills. Review and discuss teacher's observations and add information from your observations of the child. Assist teacher in designing activities, props, or interest areas that promote literacy.

Module 6: Communication (continued)

Learning Activity	What Teachers Do	What Trainers Do
Summarizing Your Progress	Review and add examples to charts from Learning Activity I. Review responses to pre-training assessment, summarize what was learned in this module, and list skills developed or improved.	Discuss summary of progress. Schedule assessments for this module.

Strategies for Extending Learning

- Ask teachers if you can audio- or videotape their conversations with children. Listen to or view the tape together and discuss ways to encourage children's listening and speaking skills.

- Offer a workshop on signs of a possible speech or language delay or disability. Work with the program director to establish a system for informing parents of teachers' observations and making referrals to speech and language specialists, if necessary.

- During visits to classrooms, model your own love of reading by reading aloud to children, individually or in small groups.

- Invite a local librarian to visit the program to share information about library books and services for preschool children.

- Work with teachers to plan a workshop for parents on creating home literacy environments that naturally encourage children to explore reading and writing.

- Collect literacy-related materials such as food containers, signs, travel posters, calendars, magazines, phone books and message pads, in English and children's home languages. Have teachers brainstorm how to organize and display the materials to encourage children to explore literacy skills in their play.

Completing Module 7: Creative

Learning Activity	What Teachers Do	What Trainers Do
Overview and Pre-Training Assessment	Read about creativity and what teachers can do to promote preschool children's creativity. Read examples of situations in which teachers promoted children's creativity and answer questions. Complete several exercises to stimulate creative thinking. Complete pre-training assessment and list three to five skills to improve or topics to learn more about. Discuss overview and pre-training assessment with the trainer.	Review their ongoing written observations of teachers. Discuss with teachers: responses to questions; responses to creative thinking exercises and how they relate to encouraging children's creativity; and pre-training assessment. Validate pre-training assessment where possible with their written observations.
I. Using Your Knowledge of Child Development to Encourage Children's Creativity	Read about the ways preschool children use small muscles, thinking, language, and social skills to explore creativity. Complete a three-day log describing words and actions used to encourage children's creativity. Discuss the activity with the trainer.	Share observations of teachers promoting children's creativity. Review and discuss three-day logs. Suggest additional ways to support children's creativity through words and actions.
II. Providing an Environment That Supports Creativity	Read about how materials and activities can encourage children to be creative in all interest areas. Use a checklist to assess whether the environment encourages creativity. Explain each rating. Share the assessment results with colleagues and plan ways to improve the environment.	Review completed checklists and offer feedback and additional suggestions. If appropriate, attend the meeting with colleagues and help teachers implement their improvement plans.

Module 7: Creative (continued)

Learning Activity	What Teachers Do	What Trainers Do
III. Promoting Creativity Through Interactions with Children	Read about teacher interactions that let children know their creativity is valued. Read also about asking open-ended questions to encourage children's creativity. Use a checklist to assess whether their teaching practices encourage creativity. Explain each rating. Share assessment results with colleagues and encourage them to continue using teaching practices that encourage creativity.	Review completed checklists and offer feedback and additional suggestions. If appropriate, attend the meeting with colleagues. Observe teachers and share specific examples from their notes of how teachers' interactions with children encourage creativity.
IV. Encouraging Self-Expression Though Music and Movement Experiences	Read about listening to sounds and music, singing with children, playing with rhythm instruments, and encouraging creative movement. With a colleague, plan improved strategies for using different kinds of music and movement experiences. Select one strategy to implement. Report on what happened. Discuss the activity with the trainer. Work with colleagues to implement the other strategies.	Review and discuss improvement strategies and report of what happened while trying one strategy over a week-long period. Discuss ways children can express their creativity through music and movement experiences.
V. Offering Art Experiences That Invite Exploration and Experimentation	Read about why children enjoy the process of using art materials; art activities offered every day; developmental stages of drawing and painting; paints, painting tools, and paper; collages and assemblages; and playdough and clay. Review a chart of suggested art materials. Observe a child engaged in art experiences over a three-day period. Use notes to select, plan, and implement an art activity to match the child's interest and skill level. Report on what happened. Discuss the activity with the trainer.	Help teachers plan ways to provide a variety of open-ended art materials and experiences that allow children to fully explore the creative process. Review and discuss observation notes and activity plan. If possible, observe teachers implementing the activity. Assist in cleaning up after messy activities. Model ways to include children in clean up—sweeping, mopping, wiping tables, and so on.

Module 7: Creative (continued)

Learning Activity	What Teachers Do	What Trainers Do
Summarizing Your Progress	Review responses to pre-training assessment, summarize what was learned in this module, and list skills developed or improved.	Discuss summary of progress. Schedule assessments for this module.

Strategies for Extending Learning

• Offer a hands-on, open-ended workshop on the creative process. Provide a wide variety of materials and encourage teachers to get fully involved. Help teachers focus on the process rather than the products of their creative work. At the end of the workshop, ask participants to discuss their feelings about staying focused on the process of creativity. How might their experiences affect their approach to encouraging children's creativity?

• Encourage teachers to identify what they really love to do and plan ways to explore their creativity in these areas.

• Ask teachers to think of a time during their childhood when an adult supported their creativity. List what the adults did to encourage creativity. Next, ask teachers to think of a time when an adult prevented them from being creative. List the adult actions that got in the way of their creativity. Use the two lists to discuss how teachers can actively encourage children's creative efforts.

• Ask teachers to record each child's creative activities in a portfolio. The portfolio can include paintings and drawings, photographs of block structures or play dough creations, and audiotapes of singing or making music. Teachers and parents can write brief notes describing children's use of creative thinking and problem-solving skills. Remind teachers to review the portfolios periodically and share them with parents.

Completing Module 8: Self

Learning Activity	What Teachers Do	What Trainers Do
Overview and Pre-Training Assessment	Read about how children develop a sense of self and what teachers can do to support this process. Read examples of situations in which teachers fostered children's sense of competence and esteem and answer questions. Answer questions about the experiences that contributed to their own sense of self and values. Complete pre-training assessment and list three to five skills to improve or topics to learn more about. Discuss overview and pre-training assessment with the trainer.	Review their ongoing written observations of teachers. Discuss with teachers: responses to questions; experiences that contributed to their values, expectations, and sense of self and how they relate to helping children feel good about themselves; and pre-training assessment. Validate pre-training assessment where possible with their written observations.
I. Using Your Knowledge of Child Development to Foster Self-Esteem	Read about Erikson's stages of emotional development and what teachers can do to encourage preschool children's initiative. Complete chart showing how teachers can use information about what children are like to foster self-esteem. Discuss chart with the trainer. Continue adding to the chart while working on the module.	Discuss what teachers can do to help children gain a sense of self and self-esteem. Review examples recorded on charts. Share their observations of children gaining self-confidence. Encourage teachers to add to the chart while working on the module.
II. Getting to Know Each Child	Read about strategies for getting to know and understand what makes each child unique. Conduct brief observations of two children. Use notes to answer questions about each child's sense of self and self-esteem and how the children are similar and different. Discuss the activity with the trainer.	Review and discuss observation notes and responses to questions. Stress that because children's interests, strengths, and needs change quickly, regular observations are crucial. Encourage teachers to work with colleagues to create a system for conducting regular observations of each child.

Module 8: Self (continued)

Learning Activity	What Teachers Do	What Trainers Do
III. Responding to Each Child as an Individual	Read about how children develop a sense of competence that contributes to self-esteem. Read also about teaching practices that support each child as unique. Observe the same two children as in the previous activity. Use notes to describe each child and plan ways to encourage each one's sense of competence. Discuss the activity with colleagues and plan ways to respond to each child through the environment, activities, and interactions.	If possible, observe the same children that teachers observed. Discuss descriptions of children and plans for encouraging competence. Help teachers assess the environment, activities, and interactions to determine whether these contribute to children's sense of competence. Suggest ways to tailor the level of support offered to each child.
IV. Helping Children Deal with Separation	Read about the lifelong process of separation, how children cope with feelings about separation, and how teachers can work with families to help children handle separation. Select two different children, describe each child's behaviors, and plan ways to help each child deal with feelings about separation.	Review and discuss summaries of each child and strategies for helping them cope with separation. Help teachers understand that feelings about separation arise throughout the day, not just at drop-off and pick-up times.
V. Using Caring Words that Help Foster Self-Esteem	Read about the importance of showing respect for children by listening carefully to what they say and using positive and supportive words when talking with them. Write what a teacher might say to children in typical situations. Discuss the caring words with the trainer. Display caring words in the classroom, if desired. If possible, make an audio- or videotape while talking with children. Review the tape with the trainer and discuss children's reactions.	Acknowledge use of caring words. Provide encouragement and feedback as teachers begin to use caring words. Offer feedback and model speaking to children in respectful ways. Help interested teachers gain access to a tape recorder or video camera. Discuss written responses to children in typical situations. If necessary, help teachers rewrite them in positive terms. Encourage teachers to make and display several signs listing caring words to use as reminders.

Module 8: Self (continued)

Learning Activity	What Teachers Do	What Trainers Do
Summarizing Your Progress	Review and add examples to charts from Learning Activity I. Review responses to pre-training assessment, summarize what was learned in this module, and list skills developed or improved.	Discuss summary of progress. Schedule assessments for this module.

Strategies for Extending Learning

- Ask teachers to suggest new materials that would offer greater challenges, allow children to use skills they aren't currently using, provide greater variety, or respond to children's families, ethnicity, cultures, home languages, and other individual characteristics. Collect items such as dramatic play props, and set priorities for purchasing others.

- Encourage teachers to share with families specific examples of their children's skills and accomplishments. Have teachers role play an instance in which they offer suggestions to parents about promoting children's sense of competence at home.

- Have teachers think back to the people whose company they especially enjoyed during childhood. Ask them to picture themselves talking with one of these people. Ask questions such as the following to lead a discussion about how adults can help children feel competent.

  - What did this person do or say to help you feel good about yourself?
  - How did you feel about yourself at the time?
  - How did your experiences with this person affect your sense of competence?
  - What can you do and say to help children feel competent of their abilities?

- Lead a discussion about daily routines—what teachers do and how they involve the children. Identify tasks the children can do alone and those that require some guidance from teachers. List materials, such as small pitchers and brooms, that allow children to do "real" jobs. Assess whether classroom arrangements are encouraging children's competence. For example, are toys, materials, and items such as tissues and paper towels stored within children's reach, so children can be independent?

Completing Module 9: Social

Learning Activity	What Teachers Do	What Trainers Do
Overview and Pre-Training Assessment	Read about how children develop social skills and what teachers can do to promote children's social skills. Read examples of situations in which teachers promoted children's social skills and answer questions. Read and reflect on the ways teachers model social skills. Complete pre-training assessment and list three to five skills to improve or topics to learn more about. Discuss overview and pre-training assessment with the trainer.	Review their ongoing written observations of teachers. Discuss with teachers: responses to questions; experiences modeling social skills and how children learn from teachers; and pre-training assessment. Validate pre-training assessment where possible with their written observations.
I. Using Your Knowledge of Child Development to Promote Social Development	Read about the role of play in preschool children's social development. Complete chart showing how teachers can use child development information to promote social development. Discuss chart with the trainer. Continue adding to the chart while working on the module.	Discuss what teachers can do to help children develop and use social skills. Review examples recorded on charts. Share their observations of children using social skills in their play. Encourage teachers to add to the chart while working on the module.
II. Promoting Children's Dramatic Play	Read about creating an environment that supports dramatic play using prop boxes. Read also about what teachers can do to guide and extend children's play. Create a prop box, observe children using the props, report on what the children did, and write a plan for extending their play. Discuss the activity with the trainer.	Offer to help collect items for prop boxes. Suggest props that reflect the children's cultures, ethnicity, families, and home languages. Review and discuss observation summaries and plans for extending play. Help teachers think of props to add to the box and other ways to build on the children's play.

Module 9: Social (continued)

Learning Activity	What Teachers Do	What Trainers Do
III. Creating an Environment That Supports Children's Social Development	Read about how features of the physical and programmatic environment can support children's social development. Select one aspect of the physical environment and one aspect of the programmatic environment. Describe how it affects social development. Then, explain how to change each aspect, implement changes, and report on what happened. Discuss the activity with colleagues. Implement other changes, as needed.	Discuss features of the physical and programmatic environments that support social development. Ask teachers to give examples of how their environments meet the criteria listed in the activity. Review and offer feedback on reports. If possible, observe in classrooms and attend discussions with colleagues. Offer to help make changes, if appropriate.
IV. Helping Children Learn Caring Behaviors	Read about how to recognize and encourage caring behaviors in children. For three days, conduct five-minute observations several times a day. Review notes and list examples of children learning caring behaviors. Reflect on their own behaviors and interactions. Note examples of times they demonstrated and promoted caring behaviors. Make and read a book to children about caring behaviors. Report on what happened. Discuss the activity with a colleague and the trainer.	Review observation summaries and discuss ways to further encourage caring behaviors. Share observations of teachers encouraging children's caring behaviors. Review and discuss the book and reading experience. Encourage teachers to continue making books about the children in their care.
V. Helping Children Relate Positively to Others	Read about the role of teachers in helping children, (especially those who are shy, overly aggressive, or rejected by others) make friends. Conduct several five-minute observations of a child who needs help learning to make friends. Review notes and summarize thoughts about the child. Use notes and information in the learning activity to plan and carry out strategies for helping the child play with others. Report on what happened. Discuss the activity with the trainer. If necessary, discuss possible causes of child's behaviors with parents.	If possible, observe in the classroom and prepare to discuss children who may be having trouble making friends. Review teachers' observation notes, plans, and results; offer feedback and suggestions. Encourage teachers to keep trying different techniques with children who are having difficulty playing with others. Check back with teachers periodically concerning children's interactions with each other.

Module 9: Social (continued)

Learning Activity	What Teachers Do	What Trainers Do
Summarizing Your Progress	Review and add examples to charts from Learning Activity I. Review responses to pre-training assessment, summarize what was learned in this module, and list skills developed or improved.	Discuss summary of progress. Schedule assessments for this module.

Strategies for Extending Learning

- Assist teachers who want to work with parents to locate professional help for a child who seems to be experiencing severe problems getting along with others.

- Suggest that teachers ask the children's librarian at their local library to recommend children's books about caring behaviors. Teachers can place the books in the library area, read them aloud to a small group of children, and offer activities and materials that allow children to fully explore the stories and characters more fully.

- Help teachers write a newsletter article or note to parents about creating and using prop boxes at home. The newsletter can describe some popular themes and props and suggest ways parents can encourage their children's play.

- Offer a workshop on play for teachers and parents. Highlight the book, *Facilitating Play,* by Sara Smilansky and Leah Shefatya and explore their theory of the relationship between socio-dramatic play and later academic achievement.

Completing Module 10: Guidance

Learning Activity	What Teachers Do	What Trainers Do
Overview and Pre-Training Assessment	Read about self-discipline and how to help children learn self-control. Read examples of situations in which teachers guided children's behavior and answer questions. Read and reflect on ways their self-discipline guides their behavior at home and work. Complete pre-training assessment and list three to five skills to improve or topics to learn more about. Discuss overview and pre-training assessment with the trainer.	Review their ongoing written observations of teachers. Discuss with teachers: responses to questions; experiences using self-discipline and how this relates to helping children gain self-discipline; and pre-training assessment. Validate pre-training assessment where possible with their written observations.
I. Using Your Knowledge of Child Development to Guide Behavior	Read about Greenspan's milestones of emotional development that are the foundation for self-discipline. Complete chart showing how teachers can use child development information to guide their behavior. Discuss chart with the trainer. Continue adding to the chart while working on the module.	Discuss what teachers can do to help children develop and use self-discipline. Review examples recorded on charts. Share their observations of teachers using positive guidance that helps children gain self-discipline. Encourage teachers to add to the chart while working on the module.
II. Creating an Environment That Supports Self-Discipline	Read about the effect of the physical environment on children's behavior. Review typical behaviors, possible problems, and solutions. List possible causes of behaviors and suggest solutions. Compare to answer sheet at end of module. For of a typical day, describe common problem behaviors, possible problems, and solutions. Discuss the activity with colleagues and the trainer.	Reflect on their observations of children's behavior. Review and discuss teachers' completed charts. After teachers make changes to the environment, conduct classroom observations. Share notes with teachers and jointly analyze the impact of the environmental changes. If misbehavior continues after teachers make changes to environment, discuss other possible causes and solutions.

Module 10: Guidance (continued)

Learning Activity	What Teachers Do	What Trainers Do
III. Guiding Children's Behavior	Read about the differences between discipline and punishment, typical reasons for misbehavior, and positive guidance approaches. Review a chart listing examples of teachers using positive guidance. For three days, keep track of how they guide a child's behavior. Report on the child's behavior, possible reasons for the behavior, and their use of positive guidance. Discuss the activity with the trainer.	Discuss the differences between discipline and punishment. Make sure teachers understand why it is important to help children develop self-discipline—a skill used throughout life. If possible, observe teachers' use of positive guidance techniques and use notes to provide objective feedback. Review observation summaries and highlight instances when teachers used positive guidance techniques. Encourage continued observation of children to determine their needs and the reasons for their behavior, and to select guidance techniques appropriate for individual children and situations.
IV. Using Words to Provide Positive Guidance	Read about the importance of words and tone of voice in guiding children's behavior and using clear, positive statements to help children understand guidance messages. Review examples of what teachers might say to guide children in different situations. Write words they could use to guide children's behavior in typical situations. Discuss the activity with the trainer. Write positive statements on poster board and hang in the room, if desired.	Read examples and discuss any that seem inappropriate. Ask, "What would a child be likely to feel or think if you said this?" Acknowledge teachers' progress in using words to provide positive guidance; give specific examples from observation notes. Review positive statement posters. Help teachers reword negative statements in positive ways, if necessary.
V. Setting Rules and Limits	Read why children need a few simple rules, how to involve children in creating rules, when rules should be individualized, using positive reminders, and revising rules as children grow. List their classroom rules and limits using positive phrases. Select one rule and answer questions about why it exists and how it is applied. Discuss the activity with the trainer.	Discuss teachers' reactions to rules—at work, at home, and in society at large—and the lessons children learn from helping to make rules. Ask teachers to describe instances when they individualized rules to meet a child's needs. Discuss the lists of rules and responses to questions. Help teachers restate rules in positive terms, if needed. Encourage teachers to set a schedule for reviewing rules to make sure they are still appropriate for the children in the group.

Module 10: Guidance (continued)

Learning Activity	What Teachers Do	What Trainers Do
VI. Responding to Challenging Behaviors	Read about children's challenging behaviors and some probable reasons for them.	Discuss the meaning of "challenging behavior" and why this term is used instead of "problem behavior."
	Focus on a child whose behavior is challenging. Describe the behavior and how teachers usually respond.	If possible, observe the child with the challenging behavior and share notes and perceptions with the teachers.
	Ask the child's parents to participate in the activity. Work with them to develop a joint plan for responding to the behavior.	If asked, help teachers prepare for the discussion with the child's parents.
	Implement the plan and evaluate the results.	Help teachers implement classroom strategies for responding to the behavior. Check back regularly to discuss the child's progress.
	Discuss the activity with the trainer.	Reinforce continued use of positive guidance to respond to challenging behaviors.
Summarizing Your Progress	Review and add examples to charts from Learning Activity I.	Discuss summary of progress.
	Review responses to pre-training assessment, summarize what was learned in this module, and list skills developed or improved.	Schedule assessments for this module.

Strategies for Extending Learning

- Offer a workshop based on strategies that help children master important socio-emotional milestones as described in Dr. Stanley Greenspan's book, *First Feelings, Milestones in the Emotional Development of Your Baby and Child* (see the bibliography in the Orientation in Volume I.) Lead role plays so teachers can practice using these strategies in a safe setting. If appropriate, model the strategies during visits to classrooms. Observe teachers using the strategies, then offer objective reports of what you saw and heard and how the children responded.

- Encourage teachers to form support groups so they can help each other plan effective responses to children with challenging behaviors. Remind teachers to maintain confidentiality related to the children and families.

- Use the information in this module and others to make a large chart showing the developmental stages of preschool children. Post the chart where all teachers can see it. Next to the chart, post a piece of paper with the question, "How can you use this information to encourage self-discipline?" Ask teachers to write their own suggestions and comment on each other's. Discuss the suggestions at a staff meeting.

- Sponsor a workshop for parents and teachers to discuss typical behaviors of preschool children and appropriate guidance techniques that can be used at home and/or at the program. Help teachers plan the agenda and select the key ideas to share with parents.

- Offer to audio- or videotape teachers' conversations and interactions with children. Listen to or view the tape together and note the words teachers used to guide children's behavior.

Completing Module 11: Families

Learning Activity	What Teachers Do	What Trainers Do
Overview and Pre-Training Assessment	Read about how teachers and parents work as a team and what teachers do in their work with families. Read examples of situations in which teachers worked with families and answer questions. Read about families and answer questions about their own experiences growing up in a family. Complete pre-training assessment and list three to five skills to improve or topics to learn more about. Discuss overview and pre-training assessment with the trainer.	Review their ongoing written observations of teachers. Discuss with teachers: responses to questions; experiences in their families and how this affects their partnerships with parents; and pre-training assessment. Validate pre-training assessment where possible with their written observations.
I. Developing a Partnership with Parents	Read about types of information that parents and teachers can share. Read also about establishing and maintaining strong partnerships with parents. For two weeks, tape or take notes on daily interactions with parents of a child. Record information shared and ways that the partnership helped the child. Discuss this activity with the child's parents with the trainer.	Observe interactions between teachers and parents. Give objective accounts of what was said and the nonverbal communication that took place. Discuss notes on interactions with family. Give feedback and suggest ways to improve the relationship, if appropriate. Suggest completing an abbreviated version of this activity with the parents of other children.
II. Keeping Parents Informed About the Program	Read about techniques for keeping all parents informed about program activities. Answer questions about a technique the program uses to keep parents informed. Suggest, try out, and report on ideas for improving it. Discuss the activity with colleagues and the trainer.	Read and give feedback on teachers' communication techniques such as newsletters, memos, handbooks, and bulletin boards. Discuss tone, language level, and sensitivity to diversity. Review responses to questions about the communication technique. Discuss new ways to keep parents informed.

Module 11: Families (continued)

Learning Activity	What Teachers Do	What Trainers Do
III. Providing Ways for Parents to Be Involved	Read about a variety of parent involvement options. Plan and try out a strategy for parent involvement. Report on what happened and develop a follow-up plan. Discuss the activity with colleagues and the trainer.	Have teachers ask parents how they would like to be involved. Discuss their responses. Review parent involvement strategies; provide reinforcement and suggestions. Offer to help get supplies if needed. Help teachers set realistic expectations for parent involvement.
IV. Planning and Participating in Parent-Teacher Conferences	Read about the goals of parent-teacher conferences and how to plan and participate in them. Prepare for a conference— complete a planning form, summarize the child's progress, and suggest goals and strategies for the next six months. Hold the conference and set goals for the next six months. Evaluate the conference. Discuss the activity with colleagues and the trainer.	Discuss the importance of holding regular conferences to review each child's progress in depth. Help teachers prepare for conferences by reviewing planning forms and role-playing what might take place. If possible, attend conferences. Then, give feedback on tone, body language, information shared, and overall success of interactions. Discuss teachers' feelings about conferences. Remind teachers that it is likely they will relate differently to each parent. Help them tailor their communication styles accordingly.
V. Reaching Out to Families	Read about recognizing when families are under stress, helping families locate resources, and providing parents with information on child growth and development. Keep a two-week journal of times they reached out to parents— list needs, responses, and outcomes. Discuss the activity with the trainer.	Review examples, offer feedback and answer questions about supporting families. Reinforce policies on confidentiality and referrals. Discuss signs of stress in children. Discuss when it is appropriate to talk about a situation with a supervisor and/or refer a family to a professional.
Summarizing Your Progress	Review responses to pre-training assessment, summarize what was learned in this module, and list skills developed or improved.	Discuss summary of progress. Schedule assessments for this module.

Module 11: Families (continued)

Strategies for Extending Learning

• Lead a discussion on the similarities and differences between the families teachers grew up in and today's families (see the overview for this module). Provide current statistics about family makeup today: single parent families; families with two working spouses; those with children from previous marriages; and families that live far away from their own parents and siblings.

• Provide information on signs and symptoms of problems faced by families (substance abuse, spouse abuse, depression). Invite appropriate agencies to make presentations on how to respond when it appears that a parent has a problem needing immediate attention. Develop a list of public and private, community and state organizations that provide services to families (e.g., hotlines and support groups).

• Work with community leaders to offer a workshop for teachers on the cultures represented in the program's families and ways to provide a program that values and responds to diversity.

• Conduct an informal survey of all parents to identify the kinds of information they would like to receive from the program and in what form (newsletters, informal chats, message centers, phone calls, bulletin boards). The survey can ask parents what information about their children they would like to share with teachers.

Completing Module 12: Program Management

Learning Activity	What Teachers Do	What Trainers Do
Overview and Pre-Training Assessment	Read about teachers' management tasks and why individualizing is an important management responsibility. Read examples of situations in which teachers effectively managed the program and answer questions. Complete a chart about ways to solve frustrating situations in their daily lives. Complete pre-training assessment and list three to five skills to improve or topics to learn more about. Discuss overview and pre-training assessment with the trainer.	Review their ongoing written observations of teachers. Discuss with teachers: responses to questions; frustrations and proposed solutions listed on their charts; and pre-training assessment. Validate pre-training assessment where possible with their written observations.
I. Using a Systematic Approach to Observing and Recording	Read about the importance of conducting observations and guidelines for systematic and objective observations. Review examples of observations that are objective and accurate and those that are not. Read about checking the accuracy of observation recordings. Observe a child for five to ten minutes each day for a week. At least twice during the week, conduct a joint observation with another person and compare recordings. If the two recordings are not similar, ask the trainer to conduct a joint observation of another child. Discuss the activity with the trainer.	Make sure teachers understand that observation is a critical skill for early childhood professionals. Teachers will use observation while completing the modules and throughout their early childhood careers. If possible, conduct and discuss at least two co-observations of the child. If this is not possible, make sure teachers conduct joint observations with colleagues or supervisors. Note examples of accurate and objective recordings that avoid the use of labels. Provide support and assistance if teachers need to repeat the activity.

Module 12: Program Management (continued)

Learning Activity	What Teachers Do	What Trainers Do
II. Individualizing the Program	Read about what it means to individualize the program, strategies for individualizing different elements of the program, and including children with disabilities. Observe two children for five to ten minutes at least once a day, for a week. Use what they already know about the children and observation notes to describe individual strengths, skills, interests, and so on. For the same two children, develop a plan for individualizing each program element. Discuss the activity with colleagues and the trainer.	Offer to supervise the children while teachers practice observing and recording. Help teachers analyze their recordings and draw conclusions about children's strengths, interest, and needs. Review and discuss individualizing summary forms and plans. Encourage teachers to establish a system for conducting regular observations of all the children.
III. Creating and Using Portfolios	Read about creating portfolios to keep track of children's skills, changing interests, and experiences that affect development. Read also about using portfolios with parents and to plan individualized programs. During a two-week period, collect items to include in a portfolio for one of the children observed in Learning Activity I or II. Involve the child and parents in selecting items. Develop a system for organizing and storing the portfolio. Report on the process. Share the portfolio with the child's parents, then with colleagues and the trainer. If desired, meet with the director to discuss setting up a system for creating, updating, and using portfolios for all children.	Review and suggest other examples of work samples and items to include in a child's portfolio. Reinforce the reasons why portfolios are effective ways to track progress and plan individualized programs. Suggest ways to involve parents and children in selecting items to include in portfolios. Discuss completed portfolios and descriptions of their contents. If appropriate, join teachers in meeting with director to discuss establishing a system for maintaining portfolios for all children.
IV. Working as a Team to Plan the Program	Read about long-range and weekly planning, weekly planning categories, evaluation, and changing plans to reflect evaluation results. Work with a colleague to develop, implement, and evaluate a weekly plan. Discuss the activity with colleagues and the trainer.	Review and provide feedback on weekly plans. If appropriate, attend planning and evaluation meetings with teachers and colleagues. Help teachers assess the effectiveness of the format and approach they now use for weekly planning. If changes are needed, offer to assist.

69

Module 12: Program Management (continued)

Learning Activity	What Teachers Do	What Trainers Do
V. Following Administrative Policies and Procedures	Read about administrative policies, practices, and procedures in early childhood programs, recordkeeping responsibilities, providing input on program issues, and laws and regulations related to including children with disabilities. Review program's policies and procedures for completing reports. Complete a schedule listing dates reports are due and teachers' responsibilities for completing them. Discuss the activity with the trainer.	Review and discuss report schedules. Discuss confidentiality issues. Help teachers schedule their time so they can complete reports and maintain records.
Summarizing Your Progress	Review observation recordings from Learning Activity I and describe how they used this information. Review responses to pre-training assessment, summarize what was learned in this module, and list skills developed or improved.	Discuss summary of progress. Schedule assessments for this module.

Strategies for Extending Learning

- Introduce a variety of observation and recording formats such as time sampling, event sampling, rating scales, and skills checklists. Encourage teachers to pick the instrument or format that best serves a particular need, such as observing to see if the environment is working, noting children's progress in a specific area, or keeping records to discuss with parents.

- Provide a video camera and tripod that teachers can use indoors or outdoors. Encourage them to let the camera run, cinema verité style. Then sit with teachers to view what the camera has recorded. Discuss what the children did, materials and skills they used, how they interacted with each other and with the teachers, and how the teachers responded.

- Organize a group of teachers to review their program's administrative policies, practices, and procedures. Ask them to suggest changes or additions to the documents to make sure they are complete and reflect in a practical way all of the program's management functions. Have group members prepare a written report and meet with the director to present their findings.

- Plan a series of workshops on the management skills teachers use such as team building, observing and recording, time management, using a planning cycle, and recordkeeping.

Completing Module 13: Professionalism

Learning Activity	What Teachers Do	What Trainers Do
Overview and Pre-Training Assessment	Read about what it means to be a professional and the four stages of professional development. Read examples of situations in which teachers maintained a commitment to professionalism and answer questions. Respond to questions about their interests and skills and how these relate to working with preschool children. Discuss responses with two colleagues. Complete pre-training assessment and list three to five skills to improve or topics to learn more about. Discuss overview and pre-training assessment with the trainer.	Review their ongoing written observations of teachers. Discuss with teachers: responses to questions; examples of times they used their special skills and interests at work and children's responses; and pre-training assessment. Validate pre-training where possible from meetings and their knowledge of teachers.
I. Assessing Yourself	Read about standards for performance established by professional associations and groups. Focus on one part of the program, and compare and contrast it with guidelines in two documents that define standards for quality. Discuss with a colleague how the standards apply to the program. Clarify their roles as early childhood professionals. Discuss the activity with the trainer.	Provide or help teachers obtain copies of documents that define standards for quality. Discuss suggestions developed by teachers and their colleagues. Help them implement suggestions, if appropriate.
II. Continuing to Learn About Caring for Children	Read about the benefits of continued learning, joining professional groups, and other ways to continue professional growth. Review responses to "Taking a Look at Yourself" in the overview to the module. Develop a plan for using available resources to improve a skill or learn more about a topic. Identify short- and long-range goals and write a plan for professional development. Discuss the activity with the trainer.	Review goals and assist in making them a reality. Periodically review progress in reaching goals and provide reinforcement and assistance. Encourage teachers to build time for training and skill development into their schedules. Provide information on relevant classes, lectures, and conferences.

Module 13: Professionalism (continued)

Learning Activity	What Teachers Do	What Trainers Do
III. Applying Professional Ethics at All Times	Review examples of the ethical standards for teaching young children as well as professional and unprofessional behaviors. List examples of ways their behavior conforms to the ethics of teaching young children. Read several ethical case studies and describe what an early childhood professional should do in each case. Discuss case studies with colleagues and the trainers.	Discuss examples of professional behavior. Review observation notes to identify and share examples of ethical behavior. Discuss ethical issues as they arise. Meet with several teachers to discuss responses to case studies. Stress that these are difficult situations and there are no easy answers. Encourage teachers by taking note of their conscientious work habits and ethical behavior.
IV. Becoming an Advocate for Children and Families	Read about the importance of advocating for children and families and how teachers can become advocates. Consider feelings about advocacy. Plan ways to become an advocate. Discuss the activity with the trainer.	Provide information on current issues related to children and families. Collect and share relevant professional articles and bulletins. Offer to assist in advocacy efforts.
V. Taking Care of Yourself	Read about the importance of taking care of one's physical, emotional, social, and intellectual well-being, and the affects of stress. Record what they did to take care of themselves for two days. Review answers after the first day and try to improve on the second day. Discuss the activity with the trainer. Plan ways to care for oneself.	Reinforce the importance of taking care of one's physical, emotional, social, and intellectual well-being. Review plans and offer to assist in implementing them. Be a good model by taking care of themselves.
Summarizing Your Progress	Review responses to pre-training assessment, summarize what was learned in this module, and list skills developed or improved.	Discuss summary of progress. Schedule knowledge assessment for this module. There is no competency assessment for this module, as the skills used are not readily observable.

Module 13: Professionalism (continued)

Strategies for Extending Learning

- Facilitate a discussion about issues affecting the health and well-being of children and families in the community or state, and discuss ways in which teachers can get involved in advocacy efforts.

- Build a comprehensive lending library of professional books, journals, and audiovisual materials on early childhood development and education, cultural competence, including children with disabilities, involving families, and other topics of interest to teachers.

- Share information about classes on stress management, nutrition, assertiveness, and other topics relevant to leading a healthy lifestyle.

- Encourage teachers to be partners in each other's professional development. They might share rides, provide child care, plan and lead workshops together, share resources, and otherwise help each other achieve their professional goals.

- Conduct workshops on ethical issues such as appropriate discipline methods or how to respond when teachers and parents disagree on practices each considers appropriate. Ask teachers to suggest topics they would like to discuss.

- Discuss with teachers the next steps in their professional development. For example, will they seek a credential, attend college courses, enroll in a degree program, or continue self-study? Help teachers understand how these modules fit into their plans for ongoing professional growth.

Chapter IV

Leading Group Training Sessions

Chapter IV

Leading Group Training Sessions

This chapter describes:

- Selecting training techniques

- Attending to logistics

- Facilitating group training sessions

- Evaluating training

- Planning a series of group sessions

- A sample training plan for Module 10, Guidance

Although *Caring for Preschool Children* is designed as a supervised, self-instructional training program, it could also be used in a variety of group settings. The modules can serve as the focus for a series of workshops offered by a resource and referral agency. Child development programs can use the modules as an in-house training program and discuss learning activities at staff meetings or at scheduled professional development sessions. Colleges can use *Caring for Preschool Children* as a textbook for several early childhood courses.

When using the modules in group settings, it is important to include regular observations of teachers working with children as a component of the training. Group meetings can provide valuable information about each teacher's progress; however, it is crucial to also offer individualized, on-site feedback and support that is based on systematic, objective observations.

If you teach a college course, observation visits can be established as a lab or practicum. Thirteen observation visits would be ideal (one per module). A minimum of eight is recommended when using these materials as the core curriculum for the courses listed in the chart on the next page. For each course, use one visit to observe and provide support and feedback and one to administer the assessments. The chart on page 12 illustrates how the 13 modules in *Caring for Preschool Children* might be used for a series of college courses.

Selecting Training Techniques

In planning group training based on *Caring for Preschool Children*, select training techniques that reflect current knowledge about how adults learn, address the needs of the teachers who will participate, and accommodate your preferences and philosophy of training. For example, if you're a skilled lecturer, you will want to include mini-lectures as part of your workshops. On the other hand, if you're uncomfortable as a lecturer, you may rely on group-oriented activities. Your choice of techniques will also reflect the preferences of those whom you are training. This means you should select techniques that suit your style and use a range of approaches to meet participants' varied learning styles.

It's best to include a variety of activities and use different kinds of media, when possible. A balance of training techniques contributes to the group's interest and ultimately ensures greater retention and application of skills and content. To encourage participants' active involvement, use role playing, small group analysis, discussion, and case studies. These techniques allow participants to apply training concepts, principles, and strategies to real-life situations.

The training techniques listed here represent a potpourri of ideas. Try out as many methods as possible to find those that suit you. Nearly all these techniques can be modified and reshaped to accommodate trainers and participants.

Written Handouts

Written material such as articles from professional journals or chapters in textbooks can be used as background reading or to provide further illustration of topics addressed in the learning activities. You can also use written materials to summarize content presented, as training assignments, or as supplemental readings for interested participants.

Audiovisuals

Audiovisuals can be very effective training tools. Videotapes that show realistic and relevant scenes from early childhood programs are especially good. Your own slides or videotapes of programs are other ways to illustrate ideas covered in training.

Overhead Transparencies

Overhead transparencies are recommended as accompaniments to presentations. They can break up the monotony of the spoken voice and reinforce the key points of a lecture for participants. Here are some suggestions for developing transparencies.

- Include key words and phrases only.
- Use large printed letters so participants can read the overheads from anywhere in the room.
- Keep illustrations or graphs simple.
- Keep color to a minimum and use to highlight, not decorate.
- Be sure there is sufficient contrast between the background color and lettering so overheads are easy to read.

Problem-Solving Activities

One of the most popular—and effective—training techniques is group problem-solving. Brainstorming solutions to realistic problems energizes a group and generates many creative ideas. The theory behind brainstorming is to separate idea creation from idea evaluation. This strategy works best in groups of 5 to 12 and requires a recorder and a moderator. The rules for brainstorming are as follows.

- All ideas are listed; no critical remarks are allowed.

- "Hitchhiking" is allowed—if one participant can improve upon or combine previously mentioned ideas, so much the better.

- "Freewheeling" is encouraged—even outlandish ideas keep the group momentum going.

- There is no limit to the number of ideas that can be included. The more ideas that participants generate, the more likely there will be some ideas that are viable solutions.

- Discussion and evaluation are postponed until participants have finished generating ideas.

Brainstorming could be used to answer questions such as the following:

- How can we involve more parents in the program?

- How can we plan open-ended activities that children can experience in different ways?

- Which community agencies and businesses could be partners with the program?

Some other problem-solving techniques you might try are described below.

- **Reverse brainstorming.** Participants identify all the negative aspects of a problem that needs to be remedied. This can be especially useful in examining current practices to see what isn't working, such as why children are getting into fights in one of the interest areas.

- **Slip method.** Participants write their solutions to a stated problem on slips of paper that are collected and grouped into logical categories for analysis and discussion. This can be especially useful in finding plausible solutions to a specific problem, such as how to keep parents informed about the program.

- **Delphi technique (group approach).** Participants generate as many responses to a particular problem as they can. Ideas are consolidated and presented for the group to consider and rank in order of viability. The filtering process identifies three to five "best" solutions to a particular problem. This can be a useful technique when participants represent a variety of roles and perspectives. For example, participants are likely to have different views and experiences related to handling a challenging behavior such as biting.

Case Studies

The chief advantage of the case study method is that it helps participants apply what they learn through lectures or assigned readings to real-life examples. By providing an illustrative story, a case study could be a powerful tool for helping participants apply theory to the real world. Many of the vignettes and examples in the modules can be used to develop case studies.

When using case studies, distribute a copy to each participant. After reading the case, participants can discuss it in pairs, small groups, or the full group. Ask questions such as the following to stimulate thinking:

- What went wrong?
- What worked well?
- How could this problem be avoided in the future?

- How could this individual build on his or her success?

- What did the children learn from this experience?

- What feedback would you provide to this individual?

Role Plays

Role plays give participants opportunities to act out real-life situations in a risk-free environment. By seeing things from another perspective, participants gain insight into various ways to approach a problem or issue. Keep in mind that some adults are very uncomfortable during role plays and may prefer to watch. Pressuring them to join in—"Oh come on, you'll have a good time"—generally backfires for both trainer and participant.

Discussion Techniques

Trainers can use the fishbowl, fantasy, and visualization techniques to stimulate discussions. For the **fishbowl**, divide participants into two groups, forming an inner and an outer ring of a circle. Give participants in the inner group an assignment based on the content presented in the training. For example, the inner group might consider how teachers can enhance their professional image. While the inner group discusses this problem for five to ten minutes, the outer group acts as observers. At the end of the allotted time, the two groups switch roles. At the conclusion of the second discussion, both groups comment on what they observed. Quite often, the discussion quickly becomes analytical because of mutual observations. This technique stimulates discussion among participants who are initially shy about contributing.

Fantasy and visualization are techniques used to draw on right brain (creative thinking) powers. **Fantasy** techniques usually ask participants to reflect on "what if . . ." situations. For example, "What if you had unlimited financial resources. How would you equip your room?" This allows participants to identify the materials and equipment in an ideal inventory. They can then compare the ideal to reality and see where compromises are appropriate. Conversely, you can use fantasy to think through worst-case scenarios.

Visualization helps participants relate the tasks at hand to past experiences. For example, you might ask participants to think about an experience in which they were forced to do something that made them uncomfortable. What were the circumstances? How did they feel? What did they do to relieve their discomfort? Did they ever get over being uncomfortable? You might use visualization if you sense that participants are uncomfortable dealing with particular situations, such as explaining to parents that children cannot attend the program when they have a contagious illness.

Mini-Lectures

These are shorter versions of lectures or oral presentations. Try to limit use of this technique to 20 minutes at a time. A straight verbal presentation is useful when you need to cover a large amount of basic material quickly. It can provide everyone in the group with a common framework.

Provide a handout summarizing the main points and let participants know in advance that this handout is available. Use visuals such as overhead transparencies or notes recorded on chart paper to illustrate key concepts. This supports the research cited earlier which says we retain 50 percent of what we see and hear compared to 20 percent of what we only hear.

At the close of the mini-lecture, review your key points, ask the group to summarize, conduct a discussion of the main points, or lead an activity related to the material covered. These steps allow participants to assimilate and make the material their own. They can relate it to their own thinking, decide what it means to them, and consider how it affects them in their work with children and families.

Group Discussions

Small groups of four to six participants are ideal for discussion and sharing. For participants who are reluctant to speak up in a large group, small group activities are a particularly good way of encouraging them to share their ideas. Small group interactions offer more intimate connections among group members, encourage the active involvement of all participants, and help them build networks and relationships.

To divide participants into small groups, try one of the following methods.

- Ask participants to sort themselves into groups of a specified size.
- Count off by a specified number.
- Distribute cards with pictures, stickers, or numbers; have participants match cards and group accordingly.
- Assign participants to groups according to roles or ability combinations.
- Distribute single parts of four to six piece puzzles—participants form groups by assembling the puzzles.
- Place pictures or names of objects that can be classified into a bag (for example, furniture, clothing, animals). Have participants choose a card then form a group with others whose objects fit in the same category.

Here are some suggestions for using small groups effectively.

- Be sure participants sit in a close circle as far as possible from other groups.
- Give three- and one-minute warnings before ending discussions.
- Ask groups to report back to the whole group "round robin" style. Each group takes a turn sharing one or two ideas until all new ideas are listed. This prevents repetitious reporting, and the first group to report does not "use up" all the popular answers.
- Reassemble as a full group without sharing what was discussed in the small groups. Reporting may not always be necessary, and not sharing discussions supports each small group's sense of uniqueness. You could suggest that the groups share their ideas informally, at break time.

Large group discussions can be used to break up a mini-lecture, discuss reactions to a videotape, and give participants an opportunity to contribute to and learn from their peers. If an entire group is 15 people or less, discussions involving the whole group allow members to contribute to and hear all the ideas presented.

The trainer's role is to facilitate communication and make sure messages are sent, received, and understood. It is important to receive participants' comments without judgment. If a statement indicates a lack of understanding, use the next break to discuss it with the participant. If a statement is incorrect, provide the correct information as diplomatically as possible, "Many people think that is true; however, the state health office recommends . . ."

During large group discussions, some participants might be frustrated because they feel ignored, misunderstood, or unable to participate. You need to observe both the behavior of the group as a whole and that of specific individuals. When a participant's comments have apparently been misunderstood, paraphrase and clarify them for the whole group. "Trinh, were you saying that . . . " This strategy allows participants to restate their comments and continue to participate.

Attending to Logistics

No matter what the topic, training is most successful when it is well planned. What may seem like simple details can enhance or destroy a training session. Here are some pointers for making logistical arrangements that support comfortable and productive training sessions.

- Schedule sessions at times that are convenient for teachers—for example, after the children leave for the day, or, if applicable, on in-service days. Teachers have steady demands on their professional and personal time. Accommodating their schedules is courteous, and it increases the possibility of high attendance.

- Notify participants of the date, time, and location of the training. If appropriate, include directions to the building and room where the session will be held. Provide an agenda and other preparatory materials in advance.

- Offer refreshments. Healthy snacks and hot or cold drinks refresh minds and energize participants. A table cloth, even fresh flowers, can make the training room inviting.

- Visit the training site to make sure the chairs provide enough support for participants to sit for a long period of time without getting restless and that there are tables or desk tops so participants can take notes.

- Prepare or arrange for needed materials and equipment in advance. This includes audiovisual equipment, videos, chart paper, markers, tape, chalk, handouts, and evaluation forms. Check to make sure the equipment works and that there are replacement bulbs, extension cords, and adapters on hand.

- Arrange the furniture before the participants arrive in a pattern that suits your training style. Many trainers prefer circles, semi-circles, or small tables because these arrangements encourage participant discussions. As a general rule, training is best received when the room is informally arranged.

- Display name tags, sign-in sheets, agendas, and reference materials in areas readily accessible to participants.

- Check to be sure the room temperature is comfortable prior to the start of the session. The temperature should be neither too hot not too cold, and air should be circulating freely. An overheated room can put an audience to sleep more quickly than a boring speaker.

By attending to these few logistical concerns, you'll be able to focus on the content of the training—rather than searching for extension cords or a building engineer to turn up the heat. Preparation goes a long way when it comes to training.

Facilitating Group Training Sessions

One of your most important roles is to help all participants feel comfortable enough to express their ideas, share their experiences, and ask questions. For some teachers, participating in group training sessions is uncomfortable. Even an experienced teacher may feel shy about talking aloud in a group. Here are some ideas you might try to help all participants share their ideas, ask questions, and offer solutions.

At the Start of the Session

- Greet participants by name as they enter. Welcome them to the session.

- Discuss the rules and guidelines, describe the plan for breaks, and state the time the session will end.

- Point out the location of rest rooms, telephones, and water fountains. This will minimize interruptions once the session starts.

- Provide an overview of the session. Explain the goals and objectives, describe the content and activities, and refer to the handouts. Invite participants to share their own expectations. Training is more effective when the group understands and shares a commitment to the goals and objectives.

- Let participants know they are responsible for their own learning. Explain that everyone will take something different from the session, depending on what is important to them, how much they contribute, and whether they integrate and use what they learn.

- Underscore the importance of the topics and skills to be covered. Emphasize that the purpose of training is to help teachers do their jobs better and enhance their professional development.

During Discussions

- Encourage participants to use active listening and to express their opinions. Acknowledge that sharing ideas and experiences in a group may feel a little uncomfortable at first. Note that all views are valuable and there is usually more than one "right" way to approach a topic. Avoid embarrassing participants by forcing each person to contribute.

- Look for "body-language" cues. They may alert you to discomfort with the subject matter (squirming), shyness about contributing (eye avoidance), or anger (turning away with the entire body). Try to respond to what you see.

- Guide participants to reach a compromise or at least respect different points of view. This is particularly important when conflicts or disagreements occur.

- Invite participants to ask questions. Answering their questions helps you explain information and eliminate misunderstandings. Before responding, rephrase the question to clarify what is being asked. Redirect some questions to the group to help participants find answers based on their own experiences and expertise. If you can't answer a question, say so and try to find out the answer. Then do it and follow up to get the answer to the participant.

- Ask questions in response to cues from the audience. At times, it is appropriate to use both direct questions ("What books do you think would be helpful to a child whose parents are divorcing?") and open-ended questions ("How would you handle that situation?"). Also, refer a question to the entire group if you sense that an in-depth discussion would be beneficial. ("That's a tough problem. Does anyone have a suggestion?")

Throughout the Session

- Draw on participants' experiences. Training is more meaningful when participants can relate concepts to personal situations and experiences.

- Emphasize skill development rather than rote learning of "correct" responses. Learning is the process of assimilating new information and using it to improve skills.

- Encourage participants to make interpretations and draw conclusions. Effective training provides background information, data, and examples participants can use to identify patterns or trends, make generalizations, and draw conclusions.

- Adjust the agenda to meet the needs of participants. Use a mixture of planned and spontaneous activities and content, just as you take advantage of "teachable moments" with children.

- Use small group activities to discuss feelings. Consider using role playing, simulations, or problem-solving assignments.

- Give clear instructions for activities. Repeat them if necessary. Move around the room to assist to individuals or groups who are confused about the task.

- Review and summarize each segment of the training before moving on to the next topic. At the end of the session lead a summary discussion and answer participants' questions.

- Be available during breaks to discuss issues and topics. Some participants may prefer to share their views with you one-on-one rather than in front of the whole group.

Evaluating Training

As a trainer, you will want to know whether you've met your goals. Did the participants increase their understanding of the content? Do they feel capable of implementing what they have learned? Do they think the session was beneficial? Did they gain skills or change attitudes?

To answer these questions, you can use group or individual training evaluations. The following are two examples of evaluation techniques that involve the whole group in offering feedback during a training session. If it appears that participants are not learning and gaining new skills, you'll want to adjust your training as rapidly as possible to address the pinpointed weaknesses.

Pluses and Wishes. On chart paper or a blackboard draw a chart with two columns. Label one "pluses" and the other "wishes." You can ask a volunteer to record participants' responses. Ask, "What did you like about this training—what were the pluses?" and "What do you wish the training had included but did not?" Responses are likely to vary from concerns about logistics, "The chairs were uncomfortable," to comments on the content, "I can use the ideas for making prop boxes immediately."

Gets/Wants Chart—On chart paper or a blackboard make a chart with four quadrants, like the axes on a graph. Label as in the following example.

Got—Wanted	Didn't Get—Wanted
Suggestions for encouraging creativity *Opportunities to learn from other teachers*	*Ideas for new materials* *Refreshments*
Got—Didn't Want	**Didn't Get—Didn't Want**
Video I'd seen before *Role plays*	

As you go through each quadrant ask participants to provide examples of parts of the training they "got, and wanted," "got, but didn't want," and "didn't get, and wanted." When you get to the last quadrant explain that this one doesn't need to be addressed because the items must be irrelevant to their jobs ("You didn't get this information and it doesn't matter because you didn't want it!"). See the chart above for examples of the types of responses participants might offer. When planning future training, you can review the responses and decide if you should continue to offer the things they "got and wanted," provide things they "didn't get and wanted," and eliminate the things they "got and didn't want!"

Individual questionnaires, completed at the end of the training or returned one or two weeks later, can help you assess which parts of the training were well received. (An example of a training evaluation questionnaire appears on page 86.) For example, did participants like group exercises but dislike the mini-lectures? Did they think too much content was presented in too short a time? Review participants' reactions to answer questions such as these:

- How effectively did the training accomplish its objectives?

- How relevant was the training to the participants' jobs?

- What changes to the training are needed?

- Do participants need more in-depth training? On what topics?

Participant evaluations are a valuable tool for assessing whether training needs have been met. As you review the results, though, bear in mind that not everyone is always going to be satisfied with training. Some variations in answers are to be expected, and you should revise your approach only if warranted.

Training Evaluation Form

Session Title: _____   **Date:** _____

Trainer: _____

	Completely	Somewhat	Not At All
A. Content			
1. Did the topics address your needs?	_____	_____	_____
2. Was the information relevant to your job?	_____	_____	_____
B. Trainer			
3. Was the trainer well-informed on the subject?	_____	_____	_____
4. Did the trainer help you learn?	_____	_____	_____
5. Was the presentation well-organized?	_____	_____	_____
C. Materials			
6. How appropriate and usable were the handouts?	_____	_____	_____
7. How appropriate were other resources such as videos?	_____	_____	_____

D. Suggestions or Comments (Indicate your likes, dislikes, and recommendations.)

E. How will you apply what you learned in this training?

Your name (optional): _____

Planning a Series of Group Sessions

As you plan a series of group sessions based on any of the modules in *Caring for Preschool Children,* think about the training techniques you will use, how you will facilitate discussions, and how you will evaluate the sessions. It may help to use a planning form to describe your approach. An example of a plan for a series of group sessions on Module 10 begins on page 88. This plam can be adapted to address individual interests and training needs. You can use Appendix A, Planning Form for Group Sessions, to plan a series of group sessions for any of the modules in *Caring for Preschool Children.*

Prior to each group session ask participants to submit their completed activities for your review and written comments (you may need to develop a system for doing this). Explain that you will return the activities, with your comments, at the end of each session. Offer to hold individual meetings or phone conferences with teachers who would like to discuss your feedback or have questions about the knowledge and skills addressed in the module.

Sample Training Plan for Module 10: Guidance

Overview

I. Open the Session

Begin with an open-ended question such as:

- What does the word "discipline" mean to you?

- How do you and your colleagues handle discipline?

- What are some difficulties you experience in guiding children's behavior?

- What guidance strategies do you find most effective?

- What does your discipline policy tell parents?

II. Discuss the Key Topics

A. Introduce the three major skills that competent teachers use to guide children's behaviors:

- providing an environment that encourages self-discipline;

- using positive methods to guide individual children; and

- helping children understand and express their feelings in acceptable ways.

B. Lead a discussion about the key topics using questions such as the following to encourage participation.

- How do children use self-discipline?

   Possible responses:
   - *To make decisions for themselves*
   - *To solve their own problems*
   - *To correct their mistakes*
   - *To do what is right without someone telling them what to do*
   - *To take responsibility for their own actions*
   - *To learn the rules for living in our society*

- What are some of the reasons children misbehave?

   Possible responses:
   - *They want to test the limits set by adults.*
   - *The program's schedule doesn't meet their needs.*
   - *The rules at home are different from those at the program.*
   - *A family situation is upsetting them.*
   - *They need attention but don't know how to ask for it.*
   - *They miss their parents.*
   - *They are tired, hungry, or ill.*
   - *They feel afraid or insecure.*
   - *They want to do things for themselves.*

III. Review the Three Sets of Examples

A. Review the examples of teachers "providing an environment that encourages self-discipline."

- Ask participants to offer examples of how their indoor and outdoor environment encourages children's self-discipline.

- Discuss the short situation and responses to the questions. Ask participants:
  - How do you feel about the way the teacher handled this situation?
  - How would you handle a similar situation in your program?

B. Review the examples of teachers "using positive methods to guide individual children."

- Ask participants to describe the positive methods they use to guide children.

- Discuss the short situation and responses to the questions. Ask participants:
  - How do you feel about the way the teacher handled this situation?
  - How would you handle a similar situation in your program?

C. Review the examples of teachers "helping children understand and express their feelings in acceptable ways."

- Ask participants what they do to help children understand and express their feelings in acceptable ways.

- Discuss the short situation and responses to the questions. Ask participants:
  - How do you feel about the way the teacher handled this situation?
  - How would you handle a similar situation in your program?

IV. Discuss "Your Own Self-Discipline"

Lead a discussion about the ways adults use self-discipline, using questions such as the following to encourage participation.

- How does self-discipline affect your own behavior?

  Possible responses:
  - *It guides my behavior at work, at home, and in society.*
  - *It helps me feel good about myself.*
  - *It lets me respond automatically because I have learned and accepted certain rules of behavior and want to avoid certain consequences.*

- How does your self-discipline affect your work with children?

  Possible responses:
  - *Modeling self-discipline helps children learn acceptable ways to behave.*
  - *Being in control of my behavior leads to greater self-esteem, which may make me more effective and skilled.*

V. End the Session

Answer questions. Return completed overviews and pre-training assessments. Schedule individual meetings or phone conferences to discuss responses and the three to five skills and topics teachers hope to learn more about.

Learning Activity I: Using Your Knowledge of Child Development to Guide Behavior

---

I. Open the Session

Ask teachers to share examples of techniques they use to guide the behavior of preschoolers.

II. Discuss the Text

Ask questions such as the following to encourage participants to discuss the text:

- How can knowledge of child development help you guide behavior?

  Possible responses:
  - *I will have more realistic expectations of children's abilities.*
  - *I can provide guidance that reflects developmental characteristics.*

- How do the milestones defined by Dr. Stanley Greenspan serve as the foundation for developing self-discipline and positive behavior?

  Possible responses:
  - *When children <u>feel secure and are able to look, listen, and be calm</u>, they can get involved in their play and activities.*

  - *When children <u>feel warm and close to others</u>, they enjoy playing alone and in small groups.*

  - *When children can <u>intentionally communicate without words</u>, they are able to accurately "read" other people's expectations, desires, and feelings and respond appropriately.*

  - *When children can <u>create mental pictures of what they want, need, or feel</u>, they have the ability to use words to express their feelings to themselves and to others.*

  - *When children <u>understand how one idea or feeling relates to another</u>, they recognize the consequences of their actions, learn to handle frustration, can wait for future rewards, and work hard at difficult tasks.*

III. Review the Activity

Reinforce the important connections between "What Preschool Children Are Like" and guidance strategies that help children learn self-discipline. Invite teachers to share examples of guidance strategies that respond to the developmental characteristics of preschoolers, as noted on their completed charts. When appropriate, offer examples from your own observations of how teachers guide the behavior of preschoolers.

IV. Offer Additional Resources/Activities

Provide poster board and markers so teachers can make charts similar to those in this learning activity. Suggest that teachers post them in an area such as the staff lounge so they and their colleagues can add additional examples of what preschoolers are like and ways to use this information to promote self-discipline.

V. End the Session

A. Give a brief overview of the next learning activity.

B. Ask teachers to draw plans of their indoor and outdoor environments, labeling features that promote children's self-discipline, and bring the plans to the next meeting. If possible, teachers could also bring photographs of the classrooms and outdoor areas used by the children.

C. Return teachers' completed activities with your comments. Offer to review and discuss these during individual meetings or phone conferences with interested teachers.

Learning Activity II: Creating an Environment That Supports Self-Discipline

---

I. Open the Session

Ask a volunteer to share an example of a problem behavior that occurs regularly in his or her program. As a group, analyze and suggest strategies for addressing the problem behavior using the following questions.

- When and where do problems occur?

- Which children are involved?

- What are the children usually doing?

- In what ways might the environment (e.g., materials, schedule, furniture arrangement) be causing the problem?

- How could the environment be changed to alleviate the problem?

II.   Discuss the Text

Ask teachers to share the plans and/or photographs of their classrooms and outdoor areas and discuss how different features promote self-discipline. Discuss the positive behaviors that different features promote. Consider making a handout of the chart.

Feature of Environment	Positive Behavior
There are individual, labeled cubbies within children's reach.	Children store and take care of their belongings and know that items in other children's cubbies are off limits.
The daily schedule is posted at children's eye level.	Children feel secure because they know when each day's activities will take place.
Paper towels, sponges, and brooms are stored within children's reach.	Children clean up after themselves.
Materials used together are stored together.	Clean-up time goes smoothly as children know where things are stored.
Materials are stored where children can reach them.	Children choose their own play materials without asking for assistance from the teachers.
There are private areas where children can get away for a while.	Children relax, take a break, regain control, relieve stress, or get away from the group for a while.
There are clearly defined spaces for different activities and clear traffic patterns.	Children get involved in their play and stay out of each other's way.
The outdoor area supports a variety of activities.	Children use their physical skills and enjoy familiar activities in a different setting.
There is space for indoor physical activities.	Children can safely use their large muscles without getting in each other's way.

III.   Review the Activity

A.   Ask teachers to share their responses to "Arranging the Environment to Promote Self-Discipline," and compare them to those provided at the end of the module.

B.   Discuss problem behaviors encountered by teachers. Have teachers suggest ways that changing the environment might eliminate such behaviors.

C.   Encourage teachers to help each other develop solutions.

IV.   Offer Additional Resources/Activities

A.   Show slides or photographs illustrating arrangements of furniture and materials that promote self-discipline.

B.   Encourage teachers to visit each other's rooms and outdoor areas and share ideas.

V. End the Session

A. Give a brief overview of the next learning activity.

B. Return teachers' completed activities with your comments. Offer to review and discuss these during individual meetings or phone conferences with interested teachers.

Learning Activity III: Guiding Children's Behavior

I. Opening

A. Begin this session by asking teachers to think about the differences between punishment and discipline. Cover these key points (page 173, Volume II).

- Punishment means controlling children's behavior through fear. Punishment makes children behave because they are afraid of what might happen to them if they don't.

- Discipline means guiding and directing children toward acceptable behavior. The most important goal of discipline is to help children learn how to control their own behavior.

B. Discuss the effects of punishment versus discipline. Cover the following key points.

- Punishment may stop children's negative behavior temporarily, but it doesn't help children develop self-discipline. Instead, it may reinforce their bad feelings about themselves.

- Children learn self-control through daily interactions with adults and each other. It takes a long time to learn self-discipline, but it is time well spent. Children who are self-disciplined tend to be more successful in school and in life.

II. Discuss the Text

Ask questions such as the following to encourage participants to discuss the text:

- What might children be expressing through their behaviors?

    Possible responses:
    - *I feel lonely because . . . .*
    - *I am angry because . . . .*
    - *I am afraid the other children will laugh at me.*
    - *I want to be good at something.*
    - *I need some limits.*
    - *I can't do what you asked me to do.*

- What are some positive guidance approaches you have used that help children develop self-discipline?

  Possible responses:
  - *Help children solve their own problems.*
  - *Anticipate problem behaviors and plan ways to avoid them.*
  - *Focus on the behavior, not the child.*
  - *Be polite to children at all times.*
  - *Gain control of your own angry feelings before disciplining a child.*
  - *Individualize rules and limits when needed to meet a child's needs.*
  - *Help children understand the consequences of their behavior and help them make amends.*

III.   Review the Activity

A. Ask pairs or small groups of teachers to share what they learned while keeping track of how they guide the behavior of an individual child. Ask them to discuss how the positive guidance strategies they used met the criteria listed below.

- They were based on realistic expectations for children's behavior.

- They reflect an understanding of child development.

- They reflect an understanding of this child's unique characteristics.

- They were individualized to match the situation and the child's skills and needs.

B. Ask each pair or group to present what they learned from their discussion. Address teachers' questions and unresolved areas of disagreement.

IV.   Offer Additional Resources/Activities

Share books such as those listed in the Orientation section of Volume I, pages 12 and 13, that reinforce the importance of using a developmentally appropriate approach to guidance. Discuss ways to involve parents as partners in helping children learn self-discipline.

V.   End the Session

A. Give a brief overview of the next learning activity.

B. Ask teachers if have access to tape players. Suggest that they tape themselves interacting with children.

C. Return teachers' completed activities with your comments. Offer to review and discuss these during individual meetings or phone conferences with interested teachers.

Learning Activity IV: Using Words to Provide Positive Guidance

I. Opening

Begin this session by asking teachers to think about when they were children:

- How did you feel when an adult yelled or used harsh words?

- How did you feel when an adult spoke quietly, using a firm tone of voice?

II. Discuss the Text

A. Ask questions such as the following to encourage participants to discuss the text:

- Why are your words and tone of voice powerful guidance tools?

    Possible responses:
    - *When children hear angry, insensitive words they may feel sad, ashamed, or angry.*
    - *When children hear caring words they tend to understand their own feelings and those of others.*

- What are some guidelines for using words to guide children's behavior?

    Possible responses:
    - *Use a natural but firm tone of voice so children feel safe and cared for.*
    - *Get close enough to children so you can speak at a normal level.*
    - *Crouch or kneel at a child's level when having a private discussion.*
    - *Look into a child's eyes and gently touch an arm or shoulder.*
    - *Give the child your full attention and make sure you have his or her attention.*
    - *Be sensitive to cultural differences.*

B. Use an example offered by a teacher, or one from your observations to demonstrate how to use clear statements to explain to children what they can and cannot do.

- Describe what happened.

- Tell the child what behavior is not acceptable.

- Tell the child what behavior is acceptable.

- Suggest a consequence and, if appropriate, a way to make amends.

III. Review the Activity

A. Have teachers work with one or two others to share their responses to the situations in the learning activity: How are the responses similar? How are they different?

B. Ask each team to present what team members learned from one another. Discuss any questions, unresolved areas, or areas of disagreement.

IV. Offer Additional Resources/Activities

If teachers have brought recordings of their conversations with children, invite them to share these with the group. Lead a discussion pointing out positive interactions captured on tape.

V. End the Session

A. Give a brief overview of the next learning activity.

B. Return teachers' completed activities with your comments. Offer to review and discuss these during individual meetings or phone conferences with interested teachers.

Learning Activity V: Setting Rules and Limits

I. Open the Session

Ask teachers to share a rule from their programs. Write the rules on chart paper. Ask:

- How do these rules help children develop self-discipline?

- How do these rules allow teachers to implement a developmentally appropriate program?

- How do you know that a rule is or is not working?

- How are children involved in setting rules?

- How do you help children understand the reasons for the rules?

II. Discuss the Text

Ask questions such as the following to encourage participants to discuss the text:

- Why is it important to have rules and limits?

    Possible responses:
    - *Rules and limits help teachers and children agree on behaviors that are acceptable and those that are not.*
    - *When they know adults will enforce rules and limits consistently, children feel safe and freer to explore and experiment.*

- Why is it important to have just enough rules?

Possible responses:
- *When there are too many rules children can't remember them and feel inadequate.*
- *When there are too few rules the children might be unsafe and the environment disorderly.*
- *Children feel a sense of mastery when they can remember and follow a few simple rules.*

- Why is it important to involve children in creating rules?

Possible responses:
- *Children are more likely to remember and follow rules they have helped to create.*
- *Children are more likely to understand why rules are needed if they helped set them.*

- When is it appropriate to individualize the rules?

Possible response:
- *"Bending" the rules may help teachers meet a child's unique needs.*

- Why is it important to review and revise the rules periodically?

Possible responses:
- *As children grow and mature they can handle more freedom, activities, and responsibility.*
- *Rules that were once needed to keep children safe may now be getting in the way of their growth and independence.*

III. Review the Activity

A. Have teachers turn the rules they listed in this activity into positive statements that remind children of what to do.

B. Ask for volunteers to share the examples of "Rules for the Preschool Room," and their responses to the questions on page 188-189 of Volume II. Stress the importance of respecting and acknowledging children's feelings.

IV. Additional Resources/Activities

Ask teachers to work in pairs to share and discuss the rules in place in their program. Have participants rewrite rules as needed to make them positive statements and to identify rules that might not be necessary or might need revisions to reflect children's growth and maturity.

V. Ending the Session

A. Give a brief overview of the next learning activity and summarizing your progress.

B. Return teachers' completed activities with your comments. Offer to review and discuss these during individual meetings or phone conferences with interested teachers.

Learning Activity VI: Responding to Challenging Behaviors and Summarizing Your Progress

I. Opening

Introduce the topic by asking questions such as the following:

- Why do we use the term "challenging" instead of "bad" or "problem" behavior?

- How do you handle challenging behaviors such as kicking, swearing, and temper tantrums?

- Have you tried any of the suggestions in this learning activity? If so, what happened?

II. Discuss the Text

Ask questions such as the following to encourage participants to discuss the text:

- What challenging behaviors have you encountered?

- What do you think the children were trying to express through their behavior?

- Have you identified any of the following reasons for the behavior?

  - is affected by a physical condition
  - doesn't know what he or she is supposed to do
  - needs more attention than he or she is getting
  - feels bored or confined
  - is seeking more control of the situation
  - feels frustrated or discouraged

- If so, how did you respond to the child?

III. Review the Activity

Ask for volunteers to discuss their experiences completing this learning activity. To maintain confidentiality, teachers should not use the child's name. Focus on the process used to identify the cause of the challenging behavior and to develop a plan for responding at home and at the program.

IV. Additional Resources/Activities

Invite a mental health specialist to your session to share strategies for helping children learn appropriate ways to express their feelings.

V.   Summarizing Your Progress

A.   Ask teachers to share something they learned while working on this module.

B.   Ask teachers to share some of the ways they adapted or changed their approach to discipline. How have children reacted? How have parents responded to the revised strategies?

VI.   End the Session

A.   Return teachers' completed activities and summarizing your progress forms with your comments. Offer to review and discuss these during individual meetings or phone conferences with interested teachers.

B.   Schedule individual meetings with teachers to review their progress and schedule the knowledge and competency assessments.

Chapter V

Assessing Each Teacher's Progress

Chapter V

Assessing Each Teacher's Progress

This chapter includes:

- Guidance on administering the knowledge assessments

- Guidance on conducting the competency assessments

- Instructions for scoring the assessment

- Strategies for discussing assessment results

- Knowledge assessments

- Competency assessment observation forms

Because *Caring for Preschool Children* is competency-based, the training program includes materials and procedures for assessing teachers' knowledge and competence. Knowledge assessments validate a teacher's understanding of the information presented in the module. Competency assessments allow the individual to demonstrate competence by applying his or her skills while working with children. For each module, the criteria for the competency assessment are drawn from the pre-training assessment, and most are observable and measurable. Modules 1 through 12 include both knowledge and competency assessments. Module 13 has a knowledge assessment only since mastery of the skills developed through this module cannot be readily determined during an observation period.

Trainers administer the assessments after teachers have successfully completed all parts of a module—the overview and pre-training assessment, the learning activities, and summarizing your progress. During individual meetings, the trainer and teacher discuss the responses to summarizing your progress and review the skills listed on the pre-training assessment for the module. You jointly discuss and decide whether the teacher is ready for assessment. (Having provided feedback on all the learning activities, you will already have a good idea whether an individual is ready.) If a teacher is not ready for assessment, you can suggest repeating one or more learning activities or provide additional training resources. If the decision is to proceed with the assessments, schedule a time to administer them.

The assessment process is designed as one more learning experience. If a teacher seems anxious explain that continued support is available if his or her performance on either assessment is not successful. Reassure the individual that there will be additional opportunities to gain the necessary knowledge and skills.

Trainers will need to maintain a supply of the assessments; therefore, it might be helpful to set up a filing system for storing copies of the knowledge assessments and answer sheets and the competency assessment observation forms.

Administering the Knowledge Assessments

The knowledge assessments are paper-and-pencil exercises that test knowledge of the information and concepts presented in the module. The questions, which are based on the overview and learning activities, include multiple-choice, matching, short-answer, and true/false formats. Most teachers will need approximately 20 to 30 minutes of uninterrupted time to complete the knowledge assessment. You can administer it before or after the competency assessment. Some trainers choose to make this an open-book test.

It may have been a long a time since some teachers have taken a test. Remind them to read each question completely before attempting to answer it. Also, suggest that they go back and review all of their answers before turning in the assessment. This should help them catch mistakes made because they wrote on the wrong line or misread a question.

Conducting Competency Assessments

A competency assessment is a scheduled, objective, and systematic observation of a teacher while he or she works with children. Each competency assessment focuses on the skills addressed in the module. The competency assessment observation forms appear at the end of this chapter. The forms for each module include two pages for notes, followed by a list of assessment criteria. There are spaces to indicate whether each criterion has been met, partially met, or not met.

Trainers can conduct the observation in the morning or afternoon, depending on the day's activities and the skills being observed, and provide feedback on both assessments immediately or the next day. The recommended observation period is one hour, but this may vary depending on the time of day, what the children are doing, and the scheduled and unscheduled activities that take place. You may want to observe at a particular time of day so you can witness a specific routine or activity (for example, you might want to observe arrival or departure times or outdoor play). For several modules the competency assessment should be conducted at a specific time.

- Module 1, Safe requires observation of an emergency drill.

- Module 11, Families, involves observation of drop-off or pick-up times.

- Module 12, Program Management includes observation of a teachers' planning meeting.

The competency assessments observation forms for Modules 1, 2, 3, and 10 begin with several items related to the environment and procedures. Trainers assess these criteria by reviewing documentation, looking at the environment, and questioning the teacher. They should be assessed immediately prior to the observation period.

Documenting the Observation

Your documentation of the observation is an important aspect of the competency assessment. It should provide a picture of how the teacher interacts with and responds to children. It is not possible to capture everything that takes place, but it is important to record as much as possible because this data will be used to determine competence. Observation notes should provide objective descriptions of what you observed so you can share specific information with the teacher.

Useful observation notes are:

- **Accurate:** Provide a factual and exact description of the teacher's and children's actions and words. Record actions and words in the order in which they happen. Be specific. Try to include direct quotes whenever possible.

- **Objective:** Include only the facts. Do not use labels, judgments, or inferences.

- **Complete:** Present a detailed picture of the setting, the number and ages of children, the teacher's actions, and the children's verbal and nonverbal responses. Note the number of children involved. Describe the area in which the action is taking place and the materials and equipment in use. Include descriptions of activities from beginning to end.

Scoring the Assessments

Most adults are eager to know the results of their work. It is important to score the assessments and share the results with the teacher as soon as possible.

The answer sheets for the knowledge assessments (see Appendix B) indicate how to score each question. When a question has more than one possible correct response, this is noted on the answer sheets. A perfect score is 100. To complete the knowledge assessment successfully, a teacher must obtain a score of at least 80 percent.

Here is a sample rating page of the competency assessment observation form for Module 10, Guidance.

MODULE 10: GUIDANCE

Prior to the observation period, assess the following criteria.

The Competent Teacher Will:

Make sure there are no safety hazards.

[ ] met   [ ] partially met   [ ] not met

Store toys and equipment on low open shelves.

[ ] met   [ ] partially met   [ ] not met

To score the competency assessment, go over your notes from the observation and others conducted in the past month. Use your notes to decide whether each criterion of competence was met, partially met, or not met. If you did not observe a criterion, leave the rating blank.

Next, review your ratings and decide if you think the teacher has successfully demonstrated competence.

Discussing the Results

Schedule a meeting with the teacher to discuss the answers to the knowledge assessment and what you saw and heard during the competency assessment observation period. Keep in mind that the purpose of the assessment process is to validate a teacher's understanding and application of the knowledge and skills presented in the module. In most cases, teachers already know if they have mastered the needed knowledge and skills. If appropriate, use the meeting as an opportunity to reassess training needs and to provide additional support.

If the teacher has achieved a score of at least 80 percent on the knowledge assessment, offer your congratulations and briefly review any incorrect responses. If the teacher has not achieved a passing score, take your time going over the questions and answers so you can assess how much support the teacher needs to understand fully the material presented in the module. As stated earlier, the goal is to ensure competence and understanding, not simply to have the teacher pass the test. You might have the teacher repeat specific learning activities or read additional training resources.

Here is a suggested approach to discussing the competency assessment results.

- **Begin by asking for the teacher's comments.** "How do you feel about what took place?" "Did everything go as you had planned?" "Were there any surprises?"

- **Sort out what went well and what problems existed, if any.** "What do you think went well?" "Is there anything you would want to do differently?"

- **Share your observation notes with the teacher.** "Let's look at my notes on what happened and see what we can learn from them."

- **Review the criteria together.** Ask the teacher to assess which skills were clearly demonstrated and which ones were not.

- **Give your decision and explain the reasoning behind it.**

  - If the teacher has clearly demonstrated competence, appears to understand the information, and can apply it consistently in working with children, offer congratulations and take a few minutes to share observations of his or her progress.

  - If the teacher has not met the criteria for competence, state your decision and explain why you think he or she needs more time to develop the necessary skills. Give examples from your observation notes. Ask what form of support would be most helpful and develop a plan to work together. Assure the teacher that he or she can redo the competency assessment after spending further time building skills.

As teachers work on other modules, consider periodically reviewing their competence in using the skills developed in previous ones. There may be times when your observations indicate that a teacher needs to repeat a module or at least some of the learning activities as a "skill refresher."

The following section includes copies of the knowledge assessments for all 13 modules and the competency assessment observation forms for Modules 1 through 12. Appendix B contains answer sheets for the knowledge assessments.

Knowledge Assessments

Knowledge Assessment

MODULE 1: SAFE

Short Answers. Complete the following exercises. Some require more than one response.

1. Below is the Code of Ethical Conduct of the National Association of the Education of Young Children (Principle 1.1)*. Briefly explain how this principle guides your daily experiences with children.

   "Above all we shall not harm children. We shall not participate in practices that are disrespectful, degrading, dangerous, exploitive, intimidating, psychologically damaging, or physically harmful to children."

2. For each of the following interest areas, list **two** ways to keep the area safe.

   Art
   a.

   b.

   Sand and Water
   c.

   d.

   Cooking
   e.

   f.

3. List **two** examples of items to check daily to maintain safety indoors.

   a.

   b.

---

* Stephanie Feeney and Kenneth Kipnis, *Code of Ethical Conduct and Statement of Commitment* (Washington, DC: NAEYC, 1990), p. 5.

4. Think of an emergency situation that might arise at the program. List two things teachers could do to keep children safe in that situation.

    Emergency situation: _____

    a.

    b.

Matching. Choose the numbered item in the right column that best matches each statement in the left column.

5. Write the number on the line.

What Preschool Children Are Like	**How Teachers Can Use This Information to Keep Children Safe**
a. ___ They have lots of energy and run, hop, and jump.	(1) Use butter knives for meals and sharp child-sized knives for cooking. Provide sturdy tools children can use with success. Store tools when not in use. Demonstrate how to use tools safely and involve children in setting safety rules. Limit the number of children in cooking and woodworking areas at one time and offer close supervision.
b. ___ They throw, kick, and catch objects.	(2) Provide an area where children can throw and kick soft objects without hurting others. Remind children to kick and throw balls and bean bags, not sand, toys, and other items that could cause injuries.
c. ___ They use tools such as knives, scissors, and woodworking equipment.	(3) Set up the indoor and outdoor areas so children can move freely without bumping into each other or the furniture and equipment. Limit running to the outdoor area or a supervised hallway, and offer frequent, positive reminders: "Walk inside." Provide energy outlets indoors such as a climber or a movement activity.
d. ___ They begin to understand cause and effect.	(4) Involve children in discussing and setting safety rules and limits— for example, height limits for block structures. Use positive statements as reminders. Point out potential hazards and discuss what might happen if they are not removed or avoided.

Multiple Choice. Write *X* on the line next to letter with the best response.

6. To keep children safe while outdoors in an electrical storm,
     a. ___   find the nearest tree to stand under.
     b. ___   cluster together.
     c. ___   find a wooden o r metal shed to go into.
     d. ___   seek shelter in a vehicle or low area.

7. To keep children safe after an earthquake,
     a. ___   turn on lights to see if anyone is injured.
     b. ___   go outside if inside a building.
     c. ___   light candles.
     d. ___   turn on a transistor radio and wait for emergency instructions.

8. When walking with children in traffic,
     a. ___   cross in the middle of the street.
     b. ___   pay attention to the younger children, let the older ones walk alone.
     c. ___   obey the traffic signals most of the time.
     d. ___   explain to the children what you are doing and why.

9. To help children learn to keep themselves safe,
     a. ___   make sure children memorize all the safety rules.
     b. ___   restrict most of the activities.
     c. ___   apply rules consistently and praise children who follow them.
     d. ___   let children make mistakes so they'll learn what will happen if they do not
                 follow the rules.

Knowledge Assessment

MODULE 2: HEALTHY

Short Answers. Complete the following exercises. Some require more than one response.

1. List **two** of the U.S. Department of Agriculture Dietary Guidelines for Americans.

    a.

    b.

2. List **two** things that you do daily to minimize the spread of germs in your classroom.

    a.

    b.

3. Explain why cooking is a good learning opportunity for preschool children.

4. Describe family-style eating.

5. List **two** things you do to promote your own health and nutrition.

    a.

    b.

6. What should you do if you suspect a child in the program is being abused or neglected?

Matching. Choose the numbered item in the right column that best matches each statement in the left column.

7. Write the number on the line.

What Preschool Children Are Like		**How Teachers Can Use This Information to Keep Children Healthy**
a. ____ They can dress themselves.	(1)	Show children you care about being healthy and eating good foods so that they will learn by imitating you.
b. ____ They learn by observing and imitating adults.	(2)	Encourage children to dress themselves. Remind them to wear jackets outdoors when it is cold so that they will not become chilled.
c. ____ They can use the toilet and wash their hands.	(3)	Remind children to use the toilet as needed. Be sure there is always a supply of soap, paper towels, and toilet paper in the bathroom so they can take care of their own physical needs.
d. ____ They can pour from small pitchers and use utensils properly.	(4)	Serve family-style meals. Encourage children to serve themselves so that they will learn how to select proper foods.

Multiple Choice. Write *X* on the line next to the best response.

8. HIV (Human Immunodeficiency Virus) can be transmitted by
   a. ____ sexual intercourse with someone infected with HIV.
   b. ____ sharing the bathroom with someone with HIV.
   c. ____ hugging and kissing an HIV-infected person.
   d. ____ being in the same room with an HIV-infected person.

9. Teachers and children should wash their hands
   a. ____ before outdoor play.
   b. ____ two or three times a day.
   c. ____ after using the bathroom.
   d. ____ only when dirty.

10. Teachers can help children develop healthy habits by
   a. ____ telling them to eat everything on their plates.
   b. ____ offering a variety of healthy foods for meals and snacks.
   c. ____ eating separately from the children.
   d. ____ cleaning up after the children.

11. A sign of possible child abuse or neglect might be
   a. ____ not buying a child the kind of shoes he wants.
   b. ____ disciplining a child firmly, but gently.
   c. ____ ridiculing and belittling a child.
   d. ____ allowing a child to make choices.

Knowledge Assessment

MODULE 3: LEARNING ENVIRONMENT

Short Answers. Complete the following exercises. Some require more than one response.

1. Describe how to arrange the environment to convey the message: "You belong here and we like you."

2. Describe what children do in one indoor interest area.

   Interest area: _____

3. Explain why and how you would like to improve an interest area in your classroom.

   Interest area: _____

4. List **two** ways teachers can help transitions go smoothly.

   a.

   b.

5. List **two** items that children might use in each of the following interest areas.

   Table Toys
   a.

   b.

   Sand and Water
   a.

   b.

Matching. Choose the numbered item in the right column that best matches each statement in the left column.

6. Write the number on the line.

What Preschool Children Are Like	**How Teachers Can Use This Information to Create a Learning Environment**
a. ____ They enjoy large motor activities such as running, jumping, climbing, and riding tricycles.	(1) Decide on jobs children can do alone or with adult help and make a job chart. Make name cards to show who has each job (for example, feeding pets, watering plants, setting tables, passing out snacks).
b. ____ They are learning to share and take turns.	(2) Provide duplicates of some popular toys and materials. Show children how long they have to wait. Use a clock or a timer, or write their names on a list to help them learn to share.
c. ____ They like to be helpful.	(3) Carefully organize materials. Put things together that are used together (for example, crayons and markers near drawing paper). Make picture labels to put on shelves to show where items belong, to help children see that everything has a place.
d. ____ They can take responsibility for keeping the classroom orderly.	(4) Set aside an indoor area for large play equipment. Plan some activities that use large muscles (for example, pounding clay or dough, woodworking). Make sure the outdoor area is safe for running and climbing.

Multiple Choice. Write *X* on the line next to the best response.

7. A good schedule for children includes
    a. ___ outdoor as well as indoor time.
    b. ___ large group activity at all times.
    c. ___ five minutes for cleaning up.
    d. ___ mostly indoor time.

8. In an environment that invites children to explore and try out ideas,
    a. ___ routines follow a consistent order.
    b. ___ pillows or a stuffed chair are in a corner.
    c. ___ child-sized furniture is provided.
    d. ___ attractive displays of materials invite children to use them.

9. If your learning environment is attractive and well-organized,
    a. ___ you may enjoy working more and your job may be easier.
    b. ___ the children will be afraid to touch anything.
    c. ___ you will have to spend many after-work hours putting things away.
    d. ___ you will spend more time on arranging things and less on developmentally appropriate activities.

10. The outdoor play area
    a. ___ should be used only during warm-weather months.
    b. ___ is for activities that call for large motor development only.
    c. ___ can be divided into interest areas for different types of activities.
    d. ___ is a place where children can take a break from the program and doesn't need teacher supervision.

Knowledge Assessments

MODULE 4: PHYSICAL

Short Answers. Complete the following exercises. Some require more than one response.

1. Explain how children's physical fitness is related to their self-esteem.

2. Give **one** example for each of the following skills:

   a. Object control:

   b. Locomotor:

   c. Nonlocomotor:

3. Give **three** examples of ways children can develop their fine motor skills in the library area.

   a.

   b.

   c.

4. Change the following into positive, encouraging statements:

   a. "You need to use your legs harder to swing. You're not trying hard enough."

   b. "You're running faster, but you still can't you run as fast as Sheila."

5. Are there any age-appropriate gross motor activities that you shy away from doing with the children? Why? What can you do to change your feelings about these activities?

Matching. Choose the numbered item in the right column that best matches each statement in the left column.

6. Write the number on the line.

What Preschool Children Are Like	**How Teachers Can Use This Information to Promote Children's Physical Development**
a. _____ They climb.	(1) Lead activities in which children can move their bodies to music with different rhythms. Teach children some dance movements and plan experiences where children can create their own movements.
b. _____ They move to music, imitate dance movements, and make up creative ways to move.	(2) Allow adequate time for children to use indoor and outdoor climbing equipment. Encourage children who are learning to climb so they feel competent and are not frustrated or fearful.
c. _____ They string beads, lace, zip, and weave.	(3) Have clay and play dough available in the art area every day. Encourage children to roll, pinch, squeeze, pound, and pull so they can refine finger movements.
d. _____ They manipulate objects with their hands and fingers to see how objects fit together and work.	(4) Provide fabric with zippers, yarn, string, laces, beads, spools, and other materials for children to practice stringing, lacing, weaving, and self-help skills.

Multiple Choice. Write *X* on the line next to the best response.

7. Which of the following is most typical of three-year-olds?
   a. ___ They like to run, gallop, and dance to music.
   b. ___ They don't like trying new things.
   c. ___ They are skillful at climbing.
   d. ___ They are well-coordinated.

8. Which of the following is most typical of four-year-olds?
   a. ___ They are well-coordinated.
   b. ___ They enjoy hopping and skipping.
   c. ___ They aren't very social.
   d. ___ They have very good fine motor control.

9. Which of the following is most typical of five-year olds?
    a. ___ They are well-coordinated.
    b. ___ Their running and walking movements may have sudden starts and stops.
    c. ___ They can walk upstairs using alternate feet.
    d. ___ They can throw and catch a ball with success.

10. What should a teacher do to encourage and guide children?
    a. ___ Compare one child's progress to another child's.
    b. ___ Help children learn to do large motor activities safely.
    c. ___ Stay away from children who attempt new skills so as not to embarrass them.
    d. ___ Tell all children they must walk the balance beam without any help.

Knowledge Assessments

MODULE 5: COGNITIVE

Short Answers. Complete the following exercises. Some require more than one response.

1. List **two** ways teachers can encourage children's problem-solving skills.

    a.

    b.

2. Define the following cognitive skills.

    a. Classification

    b. Sequencing

    c. Understanding cause and effect

3. Define the following types of play.

    a. Functional

    b. Socio-dramatic

    c. Constructive

4. List **two** materials you would include in one interest area to promote children's cognitive development. Explain why you would provide each material.

   Interest area: _____

   Materials:

   a.

   b.

5. List two props used for sand and water play. Describe how you encourage children to construct their own knowledge using these materials.

   a.

   b.

Matching. Choose the numbered item in the right column that best matches each statement in the left column.

6. Write the number on the line.

What Preschool Children Are Like	**How Teachers Can Use This Information to Promote Children's Cognitive Development**
a.___ They have rapidly expanding vocabularies—they can name many things and explain their ideas.	(1) Offer new props and materials that build on children's play themes. Create prop boxes tied to themes of interest to the children. Step into a dramatic play role to comment or make suggestions that will lead the children to a higher level of play.
b.___ They learn by using their imaginations—in dramatic play and other activities.	(2) Take children's questions seriously. Ask questions to find out what they really want to know. Give answers they can understand and ask more questions to stretch their thinking. Model ways to use books and other resources to find answers.
c.___ They believe there is a purpose for everything and ask many questions: "Why?" "How?" "What?"	(3) Provide a variety of appealing table toys and interesting materials, such as rocks, shells, buttons, and keys. Comment on what children are doing: "You made a row of red pegs." "You lined up the rocks by size, from large to small."
d.___ They learn to match, classify, and identify shape and colors by playing with toys and objects.	(4) Introduce new words for vocabulary building. Provide names for objects, feelings, places, events, and so on. Talk with children and encourage them to describe their activities, feelings, and ideas.

Multiple Choice. Write *X* on the line next to the best response.

7. A question that promotes children's thinking and problem solving is
    a. ___ What else could we try?
    b. ___ What color is this?
    c. ___ What letter is this?
    d. ___ How many apples are there?

8. Children ask lots of questions because they
    a. ___ want to keep the teacher busy answering them.
    b. ___ wants adults to think they're smart.
    c. ___ are curious and want to understand the world around them.
    d. ___ aren't very bright and can't help asking.

9. Cognitive development is
    a. ___ a set of skills learned through formal education.
    b. ___ the process of learning to think and reason.
    c. ___ the ability to take tests.
    d. ___ the collective sum of information a person knows.

10. When a child calls a worm a *caterpillar,* the child is
    a. ___ making a mistake.
    b. ___ noticing the ways in which a worm and caterpillar are alike.
    c. ___ obviously not ready to learn the differences.
    d. ___ not advanced in cognitive development.

Knowledge Assessment

MODULE 6: COMMUNICATION

Short Answers. Complete the following exercises. Some require more than one response.

1. List **two** ways teachers can encourage children to practice and expand their language skills.

    a.

    b.

2. Describe how you observe and promote children's listening and speaking skills.

3. List **two** conversation rules.

    a.

    b.

4. List **two** ways teachers can help children expand their vocabularies and understanding of language.

    a.

    b.

5. List **two** characteristics of appropriate books for young preschool children.

   a.

   b.

6. List **two** characteristics of appropriate books for older preschool children.

   a.

   b.

Matching. Choose the numbered item in the right column that best matches each statement in the left column..

7. Write the number on the line.

What Preschool Children Are Like	How Teachers Can Use This Information to Promote Communication
a. ____ They scribble and write invented letters and words.	(1) Print and post signs, job charts, and stories to provide important information. Label cubbies, containers, shelves, and interest areas. On a neighborhood walk, point out traffic signs and signs on buildings. Offer writing materials in a separate area and in all interest areas.
b. ____ They can memorize songs, poems, rhymes, and books with repetition.	(2) Ask children to read what they have written so you can understand what they know about writing. Accept their writing without pointing out mistakes or making corrections.
c. ____ They learn most rules of grammar without direct instruction. They may make mistakes because there are exceptions to a rule.	(3) Accept children's use of language, without pointing out mistakes. Restate children's words using standard language. Serve as a model for standard use of language.
d. ____ They are learning that printed words are symbols for spoken words and convey messages.	(4) Read books with repeated words and phrases again and again, until children know what comes next and join in. Ask parents to share their favorite poems, songs, and rhymes. Make up songs and rhymes about the children and classroom life.

Multiple Choice. Write *X* on the line next to the best response.

8. What is one way teachers can help children learn to use language effectively?
     a. ___ Use complete sentences and model standard use of language.
     b. ___ Gently but firmly correct a child who misuses words or grammar.
     c. ___ Arrange for children to watch television when they are not engaged in activities.
     d. ___ Do nothing special, because children will learn on their own.

9. Which of these is a sign of a possible speech disorder?
     a. ___ A child laughs a lot.
     b. ___ A child stutters every once in a while.
     c. ___ A child uses mostly vowel sounds.
     d. ___ A child speaks more than one language.

10. Which of the following is a stage in learning to read?
     a. ___ learning to recite the alphabet
     b. ___ exploring books
     c. ___ watching television
     d. ___ memorizing flash cards

11. Which is a good criterion for choosing books for preschool children?
     a. ___ Books should introduce unfamiliar topics.
     b. ___ Books should have few illustrations.
     c. ___ Books should be humorous and sometimes include surprise endings.
     d. ___ Books should be small.

Knowledge Assessment

MODULE 7: CREATIVE

Short Answers. Complete the following exercises. Some require more than one response.

1. Write a definition of creativity.

2. Describe a music and movement activity you do with children. Explain how the activity promotes their creativity.

3. List **four** items that children can use for art activities.

   a.

   b.

   c.

   d.

4. Describe something you did recently that was creative. Use your definition from question 1 to explain why your action was creative.

5. List **two** rhythm instruments preschool children enjoy using.

   a.

   b.

Matching. Choose the numbered item in the right column that best matches each statement in the left column.

6. Write the number on the line.

What Preschool Children Are Like	**How Teachers Can Use This Information to Promote Children's Creativity**
a. ___ Their small muscle skills and eye-hand coordination are becoming more refined.	(1) Observe children's dramatic play to learn what they are doing. Provide new materials and offer indirect suggestions to extend children's play or move it in slightly different directions.
b. ___ They use dramatic play as an outlet for their creativity.	(2) Provide a variety of tools and equipment such as brushes, markers, crayons, scissors, rhythm instruments, sand and water props, beads and strings, and a computer keyboard.
c. ___ They gain and use information about objects and events in the environment.	(3) Include open-ended materials that invite children to explore and make discoveries in all of the indoor and outdoor interest areas.
d. ___ They find ways to be creative in every activity and routine.	(4) Provide objects and materials that encourage children to move, dig, build, fill, empty, and use their senses to explore. Answer their many "Why?" questions. Encourage children to make their own discoveries.

Multiple Choice. Write *X* on the line next to the best response.

7. Which of the following is not a developmental stage of art?
   a. ___ making scribbles on paper
   b. ___ combining shapes in a realistic way
   c. ___ drawing basic shapes
   d. ___ coloring within the lines

8. Which of these ideas could encourage children's creative thinking?
   a. ___ telling children which of several items will sink in water
   b. ___ asking what children are doing and insisting they put things back where they belong
   c. ___ asking children what else they can do with a cup
   d. ___ having children point out specific tools

9. Which is important when planning and conducting activities that encourage creativity?
    a. ___ giving detailed instructions
    b. ___ making a model, so everyone will know what to do
    c. ___ never commenting on children's work
    d. ___ trying the activity before introducing it

10. Which of the following activities probably could be considered "creative"?
    a. ___ baking bread following a recipe
    b. ___ filling in a picture in a coloring book
    c. ___ fingerpainting
    d. ___ putting a puzzle together

Knowledge Assessment

MODULE 8: SELF

Short Answers. Complete the following exercises. Some require more than one response.

1. Write a definition of self-esteem. Then explain why it is necessary for every child to have a feeling of self-esteem.

2. List **two** ways teachers can get to know about each child.

    a.

    b.

3. Describe how the environment can help children develop independence and a sense of competence.

4. List **two** ways teachers can help children deal with separation.

    a.

    b.

5. Name **two** skills teachers should use when talking with children to build self-esteem.

    a.

    b.

6. Describe how your own sense of self and self-esteem affect your relationships with children in the program.

Matching. Choose the numbered item in the right column that best matches each statement in the left column.

7. Write the number on the line.

What Preschool Children Are Like		**How Teachers Can Use This Information to Promote Children's Self-Esteem**
a. _____ They may express feelings such as anger and jealousy by hitting or kicking.	(1)	Create an environment that allows children to take risks safely. For example, put mats under the climber so children won't be hurt if they fall. Offer new materials and activities regularly in response to growing skills and changing interests, and to expose children to new information and concepts.
b. _____ They can express feelings verbally using large vocabularies , but may also use "baby talk."	(2)	Work with colleagues to develop plans for carrying out routines that allow children to participate according to their abilities. Invite children to help with tasks such as moving furniture, wiping tables, or getting books ready to return to the library.
c. _____ They like to help during chores and routines.	(3)	Encourage children to use words, rather than physical behaviors to tell each other what they want. If needed, help children express the words that identify their feelings. Provide outlets such as clay and playdough, water play, tearing paper, or moving to music that help children manage strong feelings.
d. _____ They like to try new things and take risks.	(4)	Allow as much time as children need to express their ideas and feelings. Avoid stepping in to "speak" for them.

Multiple Choice. Write *X* on the line next to the best response.

8. What is one way teachers can build children's self-esteem?
   a. ___ They can discipline children who are becoming too independent.
   b. ___ They can expect all children to be at the same skill level.
   c. ___ They can allow children to make choices and support them when they try new things.
   d. ___ They can correct children's mistakes so they won't make them again.

9. Which of the following statements would be likely to build a child's self-esteem?
   a. ___ Do you want to sit in the corner? Then, do what I tell you!
   b. ___ Are you wet again? That's the third time I've changed your shirt this morning.
   c. ___ Everyone has accidents. Get a sponge from the sink so you can wipe your spill.
   d. ___ You are getting on my nerves. Go sit down.

10. Which of the following strategies can teachers use to help children deal with their feelings about separation?
    a. ___ Tell the children to stop fretting.
    b. ___ Make sure parents say good-bye, even if the children cry.
    c. ___ Try to make children forget about their parents during the time they're at the program.
    d. ___ Tell children they are too big to cry.

11. Why is it valuable to repeat activities so that children can practice skillls?
    a. ___ It helps keep children busy for long periods of the day.
    b. ___ It helps children feel successful and competent.
    c. ___ It is not valuable, it is boring for a child and should not be done.
    d. ___ It can harm children's self-esteem.

Knowledge Assessment

MODULE 9: SOCIAL

Short Answers. Complete the following exercises. Some require more than one response.

1. Describe **two** ways to help a shy child learn to make friends.

     a.

     b.

2. Describe **two** ways to help an overly aggressive child make friends.

     a.

     b.

3. List **two** ways teachers can help children learn caring behaviors.

     a.

     b.

4. Describe how your program's environment supports children's social development.

5. List **four** ways to extend children's dramatic play.

     a.

     b.

     c.

     d.

Matching. Choose the numbered item in the right column that best matches each statement in the left column.

6. Write the number on the line.

What Preschool Children Are Like	**How Teachers Can Use This Information to Promote Children's Social Development**
a. ____ They help to make and follow simple rules.	(1) Observe to see how often and in what situations a child is excluded by others. Help the child become a part of the group by offering an interesting prop or material to share, suggesting a role to play.
b. ____ They may exclude other children from their play.	(2) Involve children in making the rules for the classroom. Play simple games such as Lotto or Go Fish to help children learn to follow rules in play situations. Offer positive reminders: "Walk indoors, please," to help children follow rules.
c. ____ They ask many questions.	(3) Use questions to engage children in a discussion but answer those that require a direct response. Include others in the discussion.
d. ____ They gain greater awareness of the larger community.	(4) Take the children on trips to the firehouse, parents' work sites, the pet store, the library, and so on. Prepare for trips by discussing what will happen and how children will be expected to behave.

Multiple Choice. Write *X* on the line next to the best response.

7. Which of the following would best help a child learn to make friends?
   a. ___ asking the child why others won't let him or her play
   b. ___ giving the child a task that requires interacting with other children
   c. ___ suggesting the child play with the blocks instead of with others
   d. ___ telling the child to join in and tell the other children to let him or her play

8. Which of the following demonstrates use of a caring behavior?
   a. ___ fingerpainting
   b. ___ wiping up after yourself
   c. ___ giving a possession to another
   d. ___ playing with other children

9. Which of the following is not an example of the programmatic environment?
   a. ___ the daily schedule
   b. ___ activities
   c. ___ group time
   d. ___ parent's address list

10. What is one important way that children learn about how to treat others?
    a. ___ watching television
    b. ___ being told what not to do
    c. ___ watching adults interacting with other adults and children
    d. ___ memorizing rules of behavior

Knowledge Assessment

MODULE 10: GUIDANCE

Short Answers. Complete the following exercises. Some require more than one response.

1. Describe the difference between punishment and discipline. Why do you think discipline is preferable to punishment?

2. Rewrite the following statements so they provide positive guidance.

    a. "Hurry up. All the other children have their coats on."

    b. "No, your mother's not here yet. Stop crying."

3. List **four** positive guidance strategies.

    a.

    b.

    c.

    d.

4. List **two** questions you would ask yourself if a child consistently misbehaves. Then, explain how you would find the answers to the questions.

    a.

    b.

5. Describe a challenging behavior that one child in your program displayed and how you helped him or her learn positive ways to behave.

Matching. Choose the numbered item in the right column that best matches the statement in the left column.

6. Write the number on the line.

What Preschool Children Are Like	**How Teachers Can Use This Information to Guide Children's Behavior**
a. _____ They sometimes lose control; they may scream or strike out in anger at children or adults.	(1) Notice and comment on children's positive behaviors and accomplishments, such as participating in clean-up, helping a friend, or finishing a difficult puzzle. Try to spend some one-on-one time with each child evey day.
b. _____ They may swear or use bathroom words to get attention or without knowing their meaning.	(2) Ask children to help you do real chores so they feel useful and competent. Create situations in which children can be leaders: choosing a book for story time; teaching another child how to do something; ringing the bell to let the group know it is almost time to go outdoors.
c. _____ They like to feel powerful and important and they can be bossy.	(3) Step in immediately to stop the hitting or kicking. Calmly, but firmly say, "Hitting hurts. It's not okay to hit. Use your words to tell him how you feel." Stay with a child until he or she has calmed down and can listen.
d. _____ They seek adult attention and approval.	(4) It depends on the reasons why children are using these words. Calmly say, "We don't use those words here," and go on to something else. If children seem to be seeking attention, try ignoring them when they use the words. Provide the needed attention at another time.

Multiple Choice. Write *X* on the line next to the best response.

7. The most important goal of discipline is to
      a. ___ make children behave.
      b. ___ get children to do what adults tell them.
      c. ___ help children develop inner controls.
      d. ___ teach behaviors needed for reading.

8. People who are self-disciplined can
      a. ___ make other people behave.
      b. ___ accept the results of their actions.
      c. ___ rationalize their own behavior.
      d. ___ be bossy.

9. Teachers can provide positive guidance by
      a. ___ telling children to be ashamed of themselves.
      b. ___ sticking to a strict schedule for eating, sleeping, and playing.
      c. ___ modeling acceptable ways to express negative feelings.
      d. ___ telling children how to behave and how not to behave.

10. When a child at the water table keeps pouring water on the floor, the teacher should
      a. ___ tell the child he can't play at the water table anymore.
      b. ___ give the child a warning about his behavior.
      c. ___ clean up the spill and make the child sit by himself for 10 minutes.
      d. ___ remind the child of the rules for the water table, then ask him to get the mop to dry up the spill.

Knowledge Assessment

MODULE 11: FAMILIES

Short Answers. Complete the following exercises. Some require more than one response.

1. List **three** kinds of information parents can share with teachers about their children.

    a.

    b.

    c.

2. List **three** things you can share with parents about their child.

    a.

    b.

    c.

3. Describe what you find most rewarding about working with parents. Explain your response.

4. List **two** ways to keep parents informed about the program.

    a.

    b.

5. List **two** ways to encourage parents to become more involved in the program.

    a.

    b.

6. Describe one step in preparing for and one step in conducting a parent-staff conference.

    a. Preparing:

    b: Conducting:

Multiple Choice. Write *X* on the line next to the best response.

7. Both parents and teachers
    a. ___ are child development professionals.
    b. ___ know exactly what the child needs.
    c. ___ have genuine concerns for the child's well-being.
    d. ___ always know the reasons for the child's behavior.

8. A major source of stress for families is
    a. ___ the weather.
    b. ___ too much food.
    c. ___ chronic illness of a family member.
    d. ___ too much television.

9. When parents ask for advice about their child, the teacher should
    a. ___ tell the parents what to do.
    b. ___ tell the parents it's against the rules to give advice.
    c. ___ encourage the parents to think about what is best for the child.
    d. ___ avoid giving any kind of answer.

10. Partnerships between parents and teachers are strengthened by
    a. ___ ongoing communication.
    b. ___ keeping the parents out of daily routines.
    c. ___ keeping the relationship as professional and distant as possible.
    d. ___ never giving advice.

True or False. Write *T* if the statement is true. Write *F* if it is false. Then for each statement that is false, rewrite it to be true.

11. _____ Parents are the most important people in children's lives.

12. _____ Teachers should not bother parents by asking them about their children's interests.

13. _____ Teachers are the experts when it comes to knowing about children.

14. _____ Parents feel more involved when they know what is happening at the program.

Knowledge Assessment

MODULE 12: PROGRAM MANAGEMENT

Short Answers. Complete the following exercises. Some require more than one response.

1. List **two** administrative policies and procedures you follow every day.

    a.

    b.

2. List **two** reasons why you observe children.

    a.

    b.

3. Explain why a portfolio is a good way to document a child's progress.

4. Choose a program element (daily schedule, materials, routines, environment, transitions, small group activities, interactions, and so forth) and explain how you can individualize it.

    Program Element: _____

    Individualizing Strategies:

5. List **two** planning categories that might be helpful for your program. Explain your response.

    a.

    b.

6. List **two** things on which you could focus during an observation of child.

    a.

    b.

Multiple Choice. Write *X* on the line next to the best response.

7. To manage a child development program, teachers use
    a. ___ any method they developed that tells them something about children.
    b. ___ a systematic approach.
    c. ___ a skills checklist that they complete at the end of the year.
    d. ___ information provided by psychologists on completing a rating scale on each child.

8. Children's behavior is observed by
    a. ___ teachers only.
    b. ___ parents and teachers.
    c. ___ all people who interact with children.
    d. ___ psychologists trained to observe children.

9. Recordings of children must be objective and
    a. ___ lengthy.
    b. ___ fun.
    c. ___ accurate.
    d. ___ spontaneous.

10. An example from an objective recording is
    a. ___ Derrick is too lazy to throw the ball.
    b. ___ Derrick is an immature boy.
    c. ___ Derrick bounced the ball three times and threw it to Mike.
    d. ___ Derrick did not like the game.

11. An example of what a portfolio might include is
    a. ___ a child's attendance record.
    b. ___ a book made by a child.
    c. ___ a list of the teacher's favorite songs
    d. ___ a copy of the program's policies and procedures.

True or False. Write *T* if the sentence is true. Write *F* if it is false. Then, for each statement that is false, rewrite it to be true.

12. ____ It is best for one person to conduct all observations of a child.

13. ____ Children are constantly growing and changing.

14. ____ To individualize, planning is not as important as being spontaneous.

15. ____ Evaluation is the first step in the planning process.

16. ____ A teacher is a manager.

17. ____ It is a good idea to inform all staff members of the plans you have made by yourself.

Knowledge Assessment

MODULE 13: PROFESSIONALISM

Short Answers. Complete the following exercises. Some require more than one response.

1. What is a professional? Why do you consider yourself a professional?

2. Why is it important to expand your knowledge and professional skills continually?

3. List **two** ways to continue learning.

    a.

    b.

4. For each category, list **two** ways that you can take care of yourself.

    a. Physically
       1.

       2.

    b. Emotionally
       1.

       2.

    c. Socially
       1.

       2.

    d. Intellectually
       1.

       2.

Multiple Choice. Write *X* on the line next to the best response.

5. Setting goals for your professional growth
   a. ____ makes you feel like you are making progress.
   b. ____ guarantees you will make progress.
   c. ____ is a waste of time when you have a lot of resources available.
   d. ____ should only include things you are already good at.

6. An example of an ethical teacher behavior is
   a. ____ avoiding children you don't like.
   b. ____ wearing comfortable old jeans and a torn sweatshirt to work.
   c. ____ comforting a child who misses his or her parents.
   d. ____ talking about a child's temper tantrums in front of another child's parents.

7. The benefits of maintaining a commitment to professionalism include
   a. ____ attending meetings.
   b. ____ helping you feel competent and effective.
   c. ____ changing your profession.
   d. ____ finding out that you have been doing everything wrong.

8. An example of unprofessional behavior is
   a. ____ arriving at work every day on time.
   b. ____ having all children do the same activities or following the same schedule.
   c. ____ completing an accident report immediately after an accident.
   d. ____ giving clear directions that show respect for children.

True or False. Write *T* if the statement is true. Write *F* if the statement is false. Then, for each statement that is false, rewrite it to be true.

9. ____ A professional is someone with specialized knowledge and skills.

10. ____ Working with preschool children is not a real profession.

11. ____ It is unprofessional to speak out against inappropriate program practices.

12. ____ Confidentiality related to families is only important within the program.

**Competency Assessment
Observation Forms**

MODULE 1: SAFE*

Page 1

Teacher: _____   Observer: _____

Date/time: _____   Setting: _____

Observation Record: _____

_____

_____

_____

_____

_____

_____

_____

_____

_____

_____

_____

_____

_____

_____

_____

---

* This competency assessment must include observation of an emergency drill.

MODULE 1: SAFE (continued)

Page 2

MODULE 1: SAFE (continued)

Prior to the observation period, assess the following criteria.

The Competent Teacher Will:

Check indoor and outdoor areas daily and remove any hazardous materials.
[ ] met   [ ] partially met   [ ] not met

Check daily to see that all electrical outlets are covered and electrical cords are placed away from water, traffic paths, and children's reach.
[ ] met   [ ] partially met   [ ] not met

Check materials and equipment daily for broken parts, loose bolts, or jagged edges and make sure they are repaired or replaced.
[ ] met   [ ] partially met   [ ] not met

Arrange the room so that there are no long or open spaces that tempt children to run and so that there are clear fire exits.
[ ] met   [ ] partially met   [ ] not met

Check safety equipment monthly to ensure it is in an easy-to-reach place and in good condition.
[ ] met   [ ] partially met   [ ] not met

Develop and post accident and emergency procedures.
[ ] met   [ ] partially met   [ ] not met

Make sure the telephone is easy to reach and is working properly.
[ ] met   [ ] partially met   [ ] not met

Know where to find parents' emergency telephone numbers.
[ ] met   [ ] partially met   [ ] not met

Maintain current emergency information on all children.
[ ] met   [ ] partially met   [ ] not met

Review your records from this observation and others conducted in the last month; score each criterion of competence that you can substantiate.

The Competent Teacher Will:

Work with colleagues to supervise all children at all times.
[ ] met   [ ] partially met   [ ] not met

Follow required recommended adult-child ratios of 1:8 for a group of 16 or 1:9 for a group of 18 preschoolers.
[ ] met   [ ] partially met   [ ] not met

Know and follow established procedures for leading children to safety during a fire and other hazard drills and in real emergencies.
[ ] met   [ ] partially met   [ ] not met

Respond quickly and calmly to children in distress.
[ ] met   [ ] partially met   [ ] not met

Take safety precautions in a calm and reassuring manner without overprotecting children to make them fearful.
[ ] met   [ ] partially met   [ ] not met

Convey to children in actions and words that the program is a safe place and that they will be protected.
[ ] met   [ ] partially met   [ ] not met

MODULE 1: SAFE (continued)

The Competent Teacher Will:

Involve children in making safety rules for indoor and outdoor equipment, materials, and activities.
[ ] met   [ ] partially met   [ ] not met

Remind children of safety rules and emergency procedures using diagrams, pictures, and words.
[ ] met   [ ] partially met   [ ] not met

Demonstrate proper ways to use potentially dangerous materials and equipment.
[ ] met   [ ] partially met   [ ] not met

Teach children how to observe safety rules when taking neighborhood walks and field trips.
[ ] met   [ ] partially met   [ ] not met

Use positive guidance techniques to respond immediately when children are involved in unsafe activities.
[ ] met   [ ] partially met   [ ] not met

Point out potential hazards so children will learn how to prevent accidents.
[ ] met   [ ] partially met   [ ] not met

MODULE 2: HEALTHY

Page 1

Teacher: _____   Observer: _____

Date/time: _____   Setting: _____

Observation Record: _____

MODULE 2: HEALTHY (continued)

MODULE 2: HEALTHY (continued)

Prior to the observation period, assess the following criteria.

The Competent Teacher Will:

Check the room daily for adequate ventilation and lighting, comfortable room temperature, and sanitary conditions.
[ ] met   [ ] partially met   [ ] not met

Provide tissues, paper towels, soap, and plastic-lined, covered waste containers in places children can reach.
[ ] met   [ ] partially met   [ ] not met

Follow a flexible daily schedule that offers a balance of relaxing and vigorous indoor and outdoor activities.
[ ] met   [ ] partially met   [ ] not met

State the definitions and describe the signs of possible physical abuse, sexual abuse, emotional abuse or maltreatment, and neglect.
[ ] met   [ ] partially met   [ ] not met

State the applicable laws and program policies related to reporting suspected child abuse and neglect to authorities without waiting for proof and maintaining confidentiality after filing a report.
[ ] met   [ ] partially met   [ ] not met

Review your records from this observation and others conducted in the last month; score each criterion of competence that you can substantiate.

The Competent Teacher Will:

Open windows or doors daily to let in fresh air if needed during observation period.
[ ] met   [ ] partially met   [ ] not met

Complete daily health checks and be alert to symptoms of illnesses throughout the day.
[ ] met   [ ] partially met   [ ] not met

Recognize symptoms of common childhood diseases and stay in regular contact with parents.
[ ] met   [ ] partially met   [ ] not met

Wash hands and make sure children wash theirs frequently using the method recommended by the Centers for Disease Control.
[ ] met   [ ] partially met   [ ] not met

Clean and disinfect table surfaces before and after preparing and serving food.
[ ] met   [ ] partially met   [ ] not met

Encourage children to use self-help skills for toileting, handwashing, toothbrushing, and at snack and mealtimes.
[ ] met   [ ] partially met   [ ] not met

Model healthy habits, such as handwashing, using tissues, eating nutritious foods, and sanitizing materials and surfaces.
[ ] met   [ ] partially met   [ ] not met

Introduce health and hygiene concepts through daily routines, conversations, books, cooking activities, and visiting health professionals.
[ ] met   [ ] partially met   [ ] not met

Plan and serve nutritious meals and snacks.
[ ] met   [ ] partially met   [ ] not met

Sit with children, "family-style," during snack and meal times to encourage conversation and to model healthy eating habits.
[ ] met   [ ] partially met   [ ] not met

Help children recognize when their bodies need a change—rest, some food or water, or movement.
[ ] met   [ ] partially met   [ ] not met

MODULE 3: LEARNING ENVIRONMENT

Page 1

Teacher: _____   Observer: _____

Date/time: _____   Setting: _____

Observation Record: _____

MODULE 3: LEARNING ENVIRONMENT (continued)

MODULE 3: LEARNING ENVIRONMENT (continued)

Prior to the observation period, assess the following criteria:

The Competent Teacher Will:

Establish a variety of well-defined and equipped indoor and outdoor interest areas that reflect children's current skills and interests.
[ ] met   [ ] partially met   [ ] not met

Create soft, cozy areas where children can play alone, look at books, listen to music, or talk with a friend.
[ ] met   [ ] partially met   [ ] not met

Define separate spaces, indoors and outdoors, for active and quiet play.
[ ] met   [ ] partially met   [ ] not met

Adapt the environment, if necessary, to fully include children with special needs.
[ ] met   [ ] partially met   [ ] not met

Provide sufficient storage for children's personal belongings, such as labeled cubbies or bins.
[ ] met   [ ] partially met   [ ] not met

Arrange the outdoor area to support a variety of activities, such as climbing, swinging, building, running, and relaxing.
[ ] met   [ ] partially met   [ ] not met

Use low, open shelves and picture labels so children can easily select materials and return them independently.
[ ] met   [ ] partially met   [ ] not met

Store materials and supplies that are used together in the same place.
[ ] met   [ ] partially met   [ ] not met

Convey positive messages through the environment (e.g., this is a safe place; you belong here; you can find what you need).
[ ] met   [ ] partially met   [ ] not met

Review your records from this observation and others conducted in the last month; score each criterion of competence that you can substantiate.

The Competent Teacher Will:

Plan a schedule that includes large blocks of time when children choose what they want to do.
[ ] met   [ ] partially met   [ ] not met

Offer a balance of activity choices including active and quiet, indoors and outdoors, and individual, small group, and large group activities.
[ ] met   [ ] partially met   [ ] not met

Display learning materials related to current activities (for example, firefighter hats, fire engines, and books on fire fighters after a trip to the fire department).
[ ] met   [ ] partially met   [ ] not met

Include dolls, picture books, photographs, and toys that positively portray different ethnic groups and people with disabilities.
[ ] met   [ ] partially met   [ ] not met

MODULE 3: LEARNING ENVIRONMENT (continued)

The Competent Teacher Will:

Provide a variety of materials to encourage dramatic play, construction, small muscle development, and thinking skills.
[ ] met   [ ] partially met   [ ] not met

Plan at least two periods a day for children to play outdoors.
[ ] met   [ ] partially met   [ ] not met

Allow time for children to use their self-help skills in daily routines such as hand washing and dressing to go outside.
[ ] met   [ ] partially met   [ ] not met

Use daily routines to teach new skills and concepts such as classification and sequencing.
[ ] met   [ ] partially met   [ ] not met

Plan something for children to do during transitions between activities so they won't be restless.
[ ] met   [ ] partially met   [ ] not met

MODULE 4: PHYSICAL

Page 1

Teacher: _____   Observer: _____

Date/time: _____   Setting: _____

Observation Record: _____

Page 2

MODULE 4: PHYSICAL (continued)

MODULE 4: PHYSICAL (continued)

Review your records from this observation and others conducted in the last month; score each criterion of competence that you can substantiate.

The Competent Teacher Will:

Encourage children to use their large muscles throughout the day.
[ ] met   [ ] partially met   [ ] not met

Play indoor and outdoor noncompetitive games.
[ ] met   [ ] partially met   [ ] not met

Encourage the development of self-help skills that involve the use of large muscles.
[ ] met   [ ] partially met   [ ] not met

Offer indoor and outdoor activities that challenge children to improve their gross motor skills.
[ ] met   [ ] partially met   [ ] not met

Provide a variety of materials and equipment that encourages all children to use their large muscles.
[ ] met   [ ] partially met   [ ] not met

Encourage children to use their small muscles throughout the day.
[ ] met   [ ] partially met   [ ] not met

Encourage the development of self-help skills that involve the use of small muscles.
[ ] met   [ ] partially met   [ ] not met

Offer activities that challenge children to improve their fine motor skills.
[ ] met   [ ] partially met   [ ] not met.

Provide a variety of materials that fit togther so children can practice their fine motor skills.
[ ] met   [ ] partially met   [ ] not met

Provide materials and activities that accommodate different fine motor skill levels.
[ ] met   [ ] partially met   [ ] not met

Encourage children to participate in daily routines.
[ ] met   [ ] partially met   [ ] not met

Offer a variety of materials and activities that encourage children of different skill levels to be physically fit.
[ ] met   [ ] partially met   [ ] not met

Schedule time for active outdoor play every day.
[ ] met   [ ] partially met   [ ] not met

Provide opportunities for indoor active play during bad weather.
[ ] met   [ ] partially met   [ ] not met

Encourage children to coordinate use of their large and small muscles.
[ ] met   [ ] partially met   [ ] not met

Help children develop an awareness of rhythm so they can coordinate their body movements.
[ ] met   [ ] partially met   [ ] not met

Introduce cooperative games and activities that build children's physical skills.
[ ] met   [ ] partially met   [ ] not met

Help older children begin learning skills they can use to play sports and games.
[ ] met   [ ] partially met   [ ] not met

MODULE 5: COGNITIVE

Teacher: _____

Date/time: _____

Observation Record: _____

Observer: _____

Setting: _____

Page 1

Page 2

MODULE 5: COGNITIVE (continued)

MODULE 5: COGNITIVE (continued)

Review your records from this observation and others conducted in the last month; score each criterion of competence that you can substantiate.

The Competent Teacher Will:

Call attention to sensory experiences as children use materials and participate in routines.
[ ] met   [ ] partially met   [ ] not met

Organize and display toys and materials logically by categories and attributes.
[ ] met   [ ] partially met   [ ] not met

Display materials that encourage children to make discoveries.
[ ] met   [ ] partially met   [ ] not met

Provide materials such as plastic bottle caps, beans, buttons, and shells that invite children to sort, classify, and order.
[ ] met   [ ] partially met   [ ] not met

Provide materials that match children's skills and interests and challenge children to extend their learning.
[ ] met   [ ] partially met   [ ] not met

Offer open-ended materials that children with varied skills and interests can use in different ways.
[ ] met   [ ] partially met   [ ] not met

Offer materials that encourage children to explore cause and effect and make predictions.
[ ] met   [ ] partially met   [ ] not met

Point out children's use of thinking skills.
[ ] met   [ ] partially met

Show children that you accept and respect their work and ideas.
[ ] met   [ ] partially met   [ ] not met

Comment on children's work in a way that introduces new words and builds on their ideas.
[ ] met   [ ] partially met   [ ] not met

Ask questions to help children recall and understand how past events relate to what is happening now.
[ ] met   [ ] partially met   [ ] not met

Answer children's questions and help them find their own answers.
[ ] met   [ ] partially met   [ ] not met

Ask questions that encourage children to think of several possible answers or solutions.
[ ] met   [ ] partially met   [ ] not met

Ask questions that help children think about cause and effect or make predictions.
[ ] met   [ ] partially met   [ ] not met

Set up activities that allow children to test out their ideas.
[ ] met   [ ] partially met   [ ] not met

Plan activities that follow up on books read with the children to extend their understanding.
[ ] met   [ ] partially met   [ ] not met

Help children apply what they have learned to new situations.
[ ] met   [ ] partially met   [ ] not met

Extend children's dramatic play by providing new props or making suggestions.
[ ] met   [ ] partially met   [ ] not met

MODULE 5: COGNITIVE (continued)

The Competent Teacher Will:

Plan activities that allow children to use their senses to explore.
[ ] met   [ ] partially met   [ ] not met

Model how to use books to learn new information.
[ ] met   [ ] partially met   [ ] not met

Help children learn about their community by taking neighborhood walks and inviting guests to visit the program.
[ ] met   [ ] partially met   [ ] not met

MODULE 6: COMMUNICATION

Page 1

Teacher: _____

Observer: _____

Date/time: _____

Setting: _____

Observation Record: _____

Page 2

MODULE 6: COMMUNICATION (continued)

MODULE 6: COMMUNICATION (continued)

Review your records from this observation and others conducted in the last month; score each criterion of competence that you can substantiate.

The Competent Teacher Will:

Accept a child's way of speaking while serving as a model for standard use of language.
[ ] met   [ ] partially met   [ ] not met

Encourage children to talk with one another by making suggestions or planning activities that will accommodate just a few children.
[ ] met   [ ] partially met   [ ] not met

Pay close attention to children's words and actions and help them express their ideas clearly.
[ ] met   [ ] partially met   [ ] not met

Make comments and ask questions that communicate interest and help children learn how to take turns in conversations.
[ ] met   [ ] partially met   [ ] not met

Stop while reading a story to talk about the characters and what they are doing.
[ ] met   [ ] partially met   [ ] not met

Be aware of signs of a possible speech disorder or hearing impairment, and discuss these observations with the child's parents.
[ ] met   [ ] partially met   [ ] not met

Learn words in children's home languages to reinforce their language development.
[ ] met   [ ] partially met   [ ] not met

Tape picture and word labels to containers and shelves where toys and materials are stored.
[ ] met   [ ] partially met   [ ] not met

Record children's words that describe their work.
[ ] met   [ ] partially met   [ ] not met

Make and post at children's eye-level signs with words.
[ ] met   [ ] partially met   [ ] not met

Involve children in making books about topics or events that are important to them.
[ ] met   [ ] partially met   [ ] not met

Show children how adults use reading and writing to learn to do a task.
[ ] met   [ ] partially met   [ ] not met

Create a well-lit, carpeted, library area with comfortable places to sit and books displayed so the covers face out.
[ ] met   [ ] partially met   [ ] not met

Create a writing area, within or separate from the library area, stocked with reading and writing materials.
[ ] met   [ ] partially met   [ ] not met

Provide props and dress-up clothes that support children's interests and emerging literacy skills.
[ ] met   [ ] partially met   [ ] not met

Teach children short poems and finger plays during transitions or activities.
[ ] met   [ ] partially met   [ ] not met

Display books, including some in children's home languages, that match children's abilities and reflect their cultures and families.
[ ] met   [ ] partially met   [ ] not met

Read to children at story times and in response to requests; invite children to retell familiar stories.
[ ] met   [ ] partially met   [ ] not met

Encourage family reading and writing times by lending books and sharing donated writing supplies.
[ ] met   [ ] partially met   [ ] not met

Page 1

MODULE 7: CREATIVE

Teacher: _____   Observer: _____

Date/time: _____   Setting: _____

Observation Record: _____

MODULE 7: CREATIVE (continued)

Page 2

MODULE 7: CREATIVE (continued)

Review your records from this observation and others conducted in the last month; score each criterion of competence that you can substantiate.

The Competent Teacher Will:

Display and store materials on low open shelves so children can easily select and replace what they need without adult assistance.
[ ] met   [ ] partially met   [ ] not met

Set up the environment so children can spread out, explore, and be messy.
[ ] met   [ ] partially met   [ ] not met

Provide sufficient space to save creations that cannot be completed in one day so children can continue to make, use, and possibly expand them.
[ ] met   [ ] partially met   [ ] not met

Help children display their own creative work attractively and respectfully.
[ ] met   [ ] partially met   [ ] not met

Display interesting pictures and objects at a child's height on the wall and invite children to explore and enjoy them.
[ ] met   [ ] partially met   [ ] not met

Adapt the schedule, when appropriate, so children's creative work is not interrupted.
[ ] met   [ ] partially met   [ ] not met

Provide books, CDs or tapes, props, and art materials in response to children's current interests.
[ ] met   [ ] partially met   [ ] not met

Offer a variety of materials, props, and real things that reflect the cultures and ethnic groups of all the children in the class.
[ ] met   [ ] partially met   [ ] not met

Encourage children to use their imaginations through activities such as storytelling.
[ ] met   [ ] partially met   [ ] not met

Avoid using coloring books, product patterns, and dittos.
[ ] met   [ ] partially met   [ ] not met

Offer "messy" open-ended activities such as water, sand and mud play, finger painting, face painting, and bubble blowing.
[ ] met   [ ] partially met   [ ] not met

Provide materials children can use in many different ways, such as blocks, musical instruments, art supplies, and dress-up clothes.
[ ] met   [ ] partially met   [ ] not met

Encourage children to express their ideas and feelings.
[ ] met   [ ] partially met   [ ] not met

Extend children's dramatic play by assuming a "pretend" role.
[ ] met   [ ] partially met   [ ] not met

Comment on children's creative thinking.
[ ] met   [ ] partially met   [ ] not met

Respect the creative process as well as the creative product.
[ ] met   [ ] partially met   [ ] not met

Call attention to sensory experiences.
[ ] met   [ ] partially met   [ ] not met

Ask questions that encourage children to solve problems and think about things in new ways.
[ ] met   [ ] partially met   [ ] not met

Accept and value each child's unique creative expression.
[ ] met   [ ] partially met   [ ] not met

MODULE 8: SELF

Teacher: _____

Date/time: _____

Observation Record: _____

Observer: _____

Setting: _____

Page 1

Page 2

MODULE 8: SELF (continued)

MODULE 8: SELF (continued)

Review your records from this observation and others conducted in the last month; score each criterion of competence that you can substantiate.

The Competent Teacher Will:

Observe each child regularly to learn about individual needs, skills, abilities, interests, culture, and family experiences.
[ ] met   [ ] partially met   [ ] not met

Encourage children to talk about their feelings and take their concerns seriously.
[ ] met   [ ] partially met   [ ] not met

Learn and use words in the home language of children whose first language is not English.
[ ] met   [ ] partially met   [ ] not met

Know what each child can do and demonstrate the belief that each child is special.
[ ] met   [ ] partially met   [ ] not met

Offer verbal and gentle nonverbal contact—a hug, a touch, a smile—to demonstrate caring feelings.
[ ] met   [ ] partially met   [ ] not met

Spend individual time with each child every day.
[ ] met   [ ] partially met   [ ] not met

Provide a variety of activities and materials that encourage all children to participate. Avoid making biased remarks concerning gender, disabilities, culture, ethnic background, or any other differences.
[ ] met   [ ] partially met   [ ] not met

Acknowledge children's efforts and accomplishments.
[ ] met   [ ] partially met   [ ] not met

Display pictures of their families and offer homelike materials and activities to help children feel secure.
[ ] met   [ ] partially met   [ ] not met

Show by what you say and do that you respect each child.
[ ] met   [ ] partially met   [ ] not met

Reinforce children's behavior when they share, cooperate, or help others.
[ ] met   [ ] partially met   [ ] not met

Make sure the environment and activities reflect the cultures of all children in the group, and help children learn about and appreciate a wide variety of cultures and ethnic groups.
[ ] met   [ ] partially met   [ ] not met

Encourage children to do as much as possible for themselves, even if this takes a long time. Provide help only when asked or when a child is anxious.
[ ] met   [ ] partially met   [ ] not met

Accept mistakes as a natural part of learning to do something new.
[ ] met   [ ] partially met   [ ] not met

Provide a range of activities and materials that can be enjoyed by children with different interests, abilities, and skill levels.
[ ] met   [ ] partially met   [ ] not met

MODULE 8: SELF (continued)

The Competent Teacher Will:

Help children learn how to solve their own problems.
[ ] met   [ ] partially met   [ ] not met

Help children handle their feelings about separating from their families.
[ ] met   [ ] partially met   [ ] not met

Repeat activities so children can master skills and experience success.
[ ] met   [ ] partially met   [ ] not met

Consider children's individual characteristics when setting up the environment, choosing materials, and planning activities.
[ ] met   [ ] partially met   [ ] not met

MODULE 9: SOCIAL

Page 1

Teacher: _____

Observer: _____

Date/time: _____

Setting: _____

Observation Record: _____

_____

_____

_____

_____

_____

_____

_____

_____

_____

_____

_____

_____

_____

_____

_____

_____

_____

_____

Page 2

MODULE 9: SOCIAL (continued)

MODULE 9: SOCIAL (continued)

Review your records from this observation and others conducted in the last month; score each criterion of competence that you can substantiate.

The Competent Teacher Will:

Encourage children to help each other.
[ ] met   [ ] partially met   [ ] not met

Include large blocks of time in the daily schedule when children can choose to play with special friends.
[ ] met   [ ] partially met   [ ] not met

Model positive ways to interact with others.
[ ] met   [ ] partially met   [ ] not met

Help children find solutions to their conflicts.
[ ] met   [ ] partially met   [ ] not met

Assist children who have difficulty being accepted by the group.
[ ] met   [ ] partially met   [ ] not met

Share personal feelings when appropriate.
[ ] met   [ ] partially met   [ ] not met

Accept children's feelings while helping them control their actions.
[ ]met   [ ] partially met   [ ] not met

Help children understand how their peers are feeling.
[ ]met   [ ] partially met   [ ] not met

State what children seem to be feeling when they are having trouble expressing their emotions.
[ ] met   [ ] partially met   [ ] not met

Give children words they can use to express how they feel.
[ ] met   [ ] partially met   [ ] not met

Read and discuss stories that help children deal with their feelings about difficult situations.
[ ] met   [ ] partially met   [ ] not met

Encourage children to work together during chores and routines.
[ ] met   [ ] partially met   [ ] not met

Establish and maintain rules and guidelines that help children learn social skills.
[ ] met   [ ] partially met   [ ] not met

Extend children's dramatic play by actively participating.
[ ] met   [ ] partially met   [ ] not met

Encourage cooperation rather than competition.
[ ] met   [ ] partially met   [ ] not met

Provide a variety of props that children can use for dramatic play.
[ ] met   [ ] partially met   [ ] not met

Provide duplicates of popular toys so children who have difficulty sharing can play together.
[ ] met   [ ] partially met   [ ] not met

Provide materials and activities two or more children can enjoy together.
[ ] met   [ ] partially met   [ ] not met

MODULE 10: GUIDANCE

Teacher: _____   Observer: _____

Date/time: _____   Setting: _____

Observation Record: _____

Page 1

MODULE 10: GUIDANCE (continued)

Page 2

MODULE 10: GUIDANCE (continued)

Prior to the observation period, assess the following criteria.

The Competent Teacher Will:

Make sure there are no safety hazards.
[ ] met   [ ] partially met   [ ] not met

Store toys and equipment on low, open shelves.
[ ] met   [ ] partially met   [ ] not met

Involve children in making up rules for the group.
[ ] met   [ ] partially met   [ ] not met

Prepare children in advance for changes.
[ ] met   [ ] partially met   [ ] not met

Arrange the materials and furniture to encourage appropriate behavior.
[ ] met   [ ] partially met   [ ] not met

Follow a schedule that allows children to initiate their own activities for most of the day.
[ ] met   [ ] partially met   [ ] not met

Review your records from this observation and others conducted in the last month; score each criterion of competence that you can substantiate.

The Competent Teacher Will:

Allow children to experience the consequences of their actions.
[ ] met   [ ] partially met   [ ] not met

Redirect children to acceptable activities.
[ ] met   [ ] partially met   [ ] not met

Help children who are screaming or thrashing regain self-control.
[ ] met   [ ] partially met   [ ] not met

Use simple, positive reminders to restate rules.
[ ] met   [ ] partially met   [ ] not met

Know when ignoring inappropriate behavior is constructive.
[ ] met   [ ] partially met   [ ] not met

Assume a firm, authoritarian role only when necessary to keep children safe.
[ ] met   [ ] partially met   [ ] not met

Make it easier to share or wait for a turn.
[ ] met   [ ] partially met   [ ] not met

Redirect an angry or frustrated child to a soothing activity.
[ ] met   [ ] partially met   [ ] not met

Tell children their feelings are accepted, even when their actions are not acceptable.
[ ] met   [ ] partially met   [ ] not met

Help children understand the effects of their actions on the environment, materials, and people.
[ ] met   [ ] partially met   [ ] not met

Model acceptable ways to express feelings.
[ ] met   [ ] partially met   [ ] not met

Work with parents to help a child with a challenging behavior learn acceptable ways to express feelings.
[ ] met   [ ] partially met   [ ] not met

MODULE 11: FAMILIES*

Teacher: _____   Observer: _____

Date/time: _____   Setting: _____

Observation Record: _____

Page 1

_____

* Conduct this competency assessment at drop-off or pick-up time. Interview teacher to verify competencies not readily observable.

Page 2

MODULE 11: FAMILIES (continued)

MODULE 11: FAMILIES (continued)

Review your records from this observation and others conducted in the last month; score each criterion of competence that you can substantiate.

The Competent Teacher Will:

Share positive and relevant information about each child's routines and activities every day.
[ ] met   [ ] partially met   [ ] not met

Respond to parents' questions and concerns.
[ ] met   [ ] partially met   [ ] not met

Suggest ways to coordinate and build on a child's home and program experiences.
[ ] met   [ ] partially met   [ ] not met

Learn parents' names and something about them as a way to build trust.
[ ] met   [ ] partially met   [ ] not met

Tailor communication strategies to meet parents' individual needs.
[ ] met   [ ] partially met   [ ] not met

Hold parent-teacher conferences regularly and as needed to share information about children's progress and to plan for the future.
[ ] met   [ ] partially met   [ ] not met

Encourage parents to visit the program at any time.
[ ] met   [ ] partially met   [ ] not met

Provide opportunities for parents to make decisions about their child's routines and activities in the program.
[ ] met   [ ] partially met   [ ] not met

Invite parents to share aspects of their culture.
[ ] met   [ ] partially met   [ ] not met

Offer a variety of parent involvement options to accommodate different schedules, interests, and skills.
[ ] met   [ ] partially met   [ ] not met

Maintain confidentiality about children and families.
[ ] met   [ ] partially met   [ ] not met

Recognize when families are under stress and offer additional support.
[ ] met   [ ] partially met   [ ] not met

Work with parents to develop strategies for dealing with a child's behavior.
[ ] met   [ ] partially met   [ ] not met

Help parents understand what their children learn through daily routines and activities.
[ ] met   [ ] partially met   [ ] not met

Use familiar terms instead of jargon when talking to parents.
[ ] met   [ ] partially met   [ ] not met

Provide parents with information on child development and typical preschool behaviors.
[ ] met   [ ] partially met   [ ] not met

Notify a supervisor when it seems a parent needs professional help.
[ ] met   [ ] partially met   [ ] not met

MODULE 12: PROGRAM MANAGEMENT*

Teacher: _____   Observer: _____

Date/time: _____   Setting: _____

Observation Record:

_____

_____

_____

_____

_____

_____

_____

_____

_____

_____

_____

_____

_____

_____

_____

_____

_____

Page 1

* This competency assessment must include observation of a teacher's planning meeting.

MODULE 12: PROGRAM MANAGEMENT (continued)

MODULE 12: PROGRAM MANAGEMENT (continued)

Review your records from this observation and others conducted in the last month; score each criterion of competence that you can substantiate.

The Competent Teacher Will:

Communicate with parents often to learn about a child's family life, culture, home language, and unique characteristics.
[ ] met   [ ] partially met   [ ] not met

Observe each child regularly and use a recording system that is objective, accurate, and avoids labeling.
[ ] met   [ ] partially met   [ ] not met

Observe children in different settings and at different times of the day.
[ ] met   [ ] partially met   [ ] not met

Collect examples and photographs of work that document children's skills, interests, and progress.
[ ] met   [ ] partially met   [ ] not met

Play and talk with children to learn about their interests and abilities.
[ ] met   [ ] partially met   [ ] not met

Meet regularly with colleagues to plan and evaluate the program.
[ ] met   [ ] partially met   [ ] not met

Use information gathered through observations to plan for individual children and the class.
[ ] met   [ ] partially met   [ ] not met

Include parents in planning for their children's growth and development.
[ ] met   [ ] partially met   [ ] not met

Use creative thinking skills such as brainstorming in planning and in solving problems.
[ ] met   [ ] partially met   [ ] not met

Change the environment, materials, interest areas, routines, and activities to address children's individual characteristics.
[ ] met   [ ] partially met   [ ] not met

Appreciate the use and strengths of all team members, including teachers, parents, and volunteers.
[ ] met   [ ] partially met   [ ] not met

Review program policies and procedures before starting a new task.
[ ] met   [ ] partially met   [ ] not met

Complete management tasks according to a schedule.
[ ] met   [ ] partially met   [ ] not met

Use the program's system for reports and recordkeeping.
[ ] met   [ ] partially met   [ ] not met

Keep informed about teachers' job responsibilities.
[ ] met   [ ] partially met   [ ] not met

Share ideas and program policies and procedures with colleagues and the supervisor.
[ ] met   [ ] partially met   [ ] not met

Answer parents' questions about program operations and refer them to the supervisor, if appropriate.
[ ] met   [ ] partially met   [ ] not met

Appendices

Appendix A

Planning Form for Group Training Sessions

Planning Form for Group Training Sessions

Use this form to plan a series of group sessions on a module. Tailor your plan to address individual interests and training needs.

Module: _____

Overview

I.   Open the Session (Ask an open-ended question to encourage discussion.)

_____

_____

_____

II.   Discuss the Key Topics

A.   Introduce the three major skills used by competent teachers.

_____

_____

_____

_____

B.   Lead a discussion by posing questions that will encourage participation.

_____

_____

_____

_____

III.   Review the Three Sets of Examples

For each set, ask participants to share examples of their own competent practices and discuss the short situations and their responses to the questions. Ask questions such as:

*   How do you feel about the way the teacher handled this situation?
*   How would you handle a similar situation in your program?

_____

_____

_____

_____

IV. Discuss the "Your Own . . . Section"

(For example, "Your Own Self-Discipline.")

_____

_____

_____

_____

V. End the Session

Answer questions. Return completed overviews and pre-training assessments. Schedule individual meetings or phone conferences to discuss responses and the three to five skills and topics teachers' hope to learn more about.

Learning Activity _____ *

I. Open the Session

Begin by asking an open-ended question, reviewing the previous learning activity, or discussing a follow-up assignment from the previous meeting.

_____

_____

_____

_____

_____

_____

_____

II. Discuss the Text

Lead a discussion focused on the key points presented in the learning activity.

_____

_____

_____

_____

_____

_____

_____

III. Review the Activity

Ask participants to describe their experiences completing this learning activity. Encourage them to share examples from their completed activities.

_____

_____

_____

_____

_____

_____

_____

* Complete one for each learning activity in this module.

IV. Offer Additional Resources/Activities

List any materials, audiovisual resources, topics for discussion, or exercises you will use to supplement the learning activity.

_____

_____

_____

_____

_____

V. End the Session

A. Give a brief overview of the next learning activity.

_____

_____

_____

B. Return completed learning activities with your comments. Offer to review and discuss these during individual meetings or phone conferences with interested teachers.

C. Remind participants of the time and place for your next session and when to submit their completed learning activities for your review and written comments.

If this is the last session for this module, discuss Summarizing Your Progress.

D. Return completed forms for summarizing your progress with your comments. Offer to review and discuss these during individual meetings or phone conferences with interested teachers.

E. Ask teachers to share one item from their summary of what they learned while working on this module.

F. Invite teachers to describe some of the ways they adapted or changed their approach to the practices addressed in this module.

G. Schedule individual meetings with teachers to review their progress and schedule the knowledge and competency assessments.

Appendix B

Answer Sheets for
Knowledge Assessments

Answer Sheets for Knowledge Assessments

Each module assessment is worth 100 points total. A score of 80 points or above is needed to pass.

There are four kinds of test questions:

1. **Short answers** Explain, identify, defend why, describe, list, and so forth in response to questions. (Give five or 10 points each, depending on the number of answers needed and complexity of the exercise. Award five points for each answer per question, or 10 points if only one answer required.)
2. **Matching** Match each numbered item in the right column with the lettered item in the left column. Write the correct number on the line. (Give 5 points for each correct response.)
3. **Multiple choice** Write X next to the best response. (Give 5 points for each correct response.)
4. **True/ false** Write T if the statement is true. Write F if it is false. Then for each statement that is false, rewrite it to be true. (Give 2-1/2 points for each correct response.)

Module 1: Safe

Short Answers

1. Answer should reflect an understanding that keeping children safe is a priority for all people who work with children.

2. Answers may include:
   a and b. locate near source of water; store scissors with points facing down; provide sponges or towels for wiping up spills; use only nontoxic materials.
   c and d. locate area away from electrical outlets and cords; limit number of children in area at one time; provide sponges or mops for controlling spilling.
   e and f. locate near source of water; have fire extinguisher near; use work surfaces at child's level; check all appliances regularly for worn cords.

3. See safety checklist, pages 44-45 of Volume I, for possible answers.

4. Answers may vary, but should include sufficient detail to indicate that teachers respond appropriately in the emergency, keeping the children's safety a priority.

Matching
5.
a. 3
b. 2
c. 1
d. 4

Multiple Choice
6. d
7. d
8. d
9. c

Module 2: Healthy

Short Answers

1. Possible responses include: avoid fats, oils, sweets; eat foods high in fiber and starch; eat at least three servings of vegetables and two fruits daily; eat lean meat, fish or poultry; use skim or low fat milk; broil or bake foods rather than fry them; use sugar in moderation; increase daily activity.

2. Answers should include two items from the health and hygiene checklist on pages 97 and 98 of Volume I.

3. It helps children develop self-help skills; improves their fine muscle coordination; increases their cognitive skills; encourages their social skills; and teaches children about good nutrition and healthy hygiene habits.

4. Answer should state that the teachers eat with the children and that everyone at the table serves themselves and engages in conversation.

5. Answers should include:
   For a and b: any of the healthful habits in the module.

6. Answer should reflect state and local laws and the program's policies and procedures for reporting suspected child abuse and neglect.

Matching
7.
a. 2
b. 1
c. 3
d. 4

Multiple Choice
8. a
9. c
10. b
11. c

Module 3: Learning Environment

Short Answers

1. Environment should include a place for children's personal belongings, child-size furniture, display of children's art work, books and other materials that reflect children's background and ethnicity, toys and materials that reflect children's interests and skill levels.

2. See pages 164-165 in Volume I for examples of interest areas and children's activities.

3. Answers may vary but should include reasons why the area needs improving and examples of changes that will make it more effective.

4. Possible responses include: give children warnings; involve children in transition activities; provide clear directions; be flexible when possible; allow children enough time to do and share work; establish a signal for quiet; keep children occupied.

5. Possible responses include:
   Table Toys— puzzle rack, beads and laces, pegs and pegboards, Cuisenaire rods, sewing cards, tinker toys, pattern blocks.

   Sand and Water—plastic pitchers, measuring cups, waterproof aprons, funnels, sponges and mops, water wheel, and eye droppers.

Matching
6.
a. 4
b. 2
c. 1
d. 3

Multiple Choice
7. a
8. d
9. a
10. c

Module 4: Physical

Short Answers

1. Answers may vary but should describe how children gain self confidence as they learn to climb, jump, and master other physical skills. Feeling competent will encourage them to try new activities.

2. Answers may include:
   <u>a</u>. kicking, throwing, catching, striking a ball with a bat
   <u>b</u>. running, hopping, skipping, balancing
   <u>c</u>. pushing, pulling, lifting

3. Possible responses include: turning pages of book, writing, placing headsets on ears, moving felt pieces on flannel board, pressing button on tape recorder.

4. <u>a</u>. Answer can vary but should not contain words that point out weaknesses or make judgments. For example, "You've almost got it. How about if I give you a push and then you can use your legs to keep going."
   <u>b</u>. Answer can vary but should not compare the child to others. For example, "You're running faster now; you keep getting faster every week."

5. Answers should reflect one or more activities that teacher has been reluctant to try, give a reason why, and propose a plan for trying to change.

<u>Matching</u>
6.
a. 2
b. 1
c. 4
d. 3

<u>Multiple Choice</u>
7. a
8. b
9. d
10. b

Module 5: Cognitive

<u>Short Answers</u>

1. Possible responses include: be patient; accept and respect children's responses; allow time for children to think; model problem-solving; encourage multiple solutions; offer help a little at a time; provide open-ended materials and toys.

2. Possible responses include:
   <u>a</u>. sorting and grouping
   <u>b</u>. putting things in order
   <u>c</u>. figuring out why things happen

3. Possible responses include:
   <u>a</u>. explore the physical properties of objects and materials
   <u>b</u>. pretend to be someone else and make believe about a situation
   <u>c</u>. use materials to create a representation of something

4. Answers should include interest area, three materials for that area, and reasons why the materials promote cognitive development.

5. Possible responses include: buckets and shovels, funnels, ladles, measuring cups and spoons, pebbles, sifter, straw, string, sponges, eye dropper, strainer, soap. bubble materials. Teachers can guide children to talk about what they are doing; do things in order; pour and measure (compare), and classify.

<u>Matching</u>
6.
a. 4
b. 1
c. 2
d. 3

<u>Multiple Choice</u>
7. a
8. c
9. b
10. b

Module 6: Communication

<u>Short Answers</u>

1. Possible responses include: set up interest areas where children can work and play together; offer interesting materials; provide dramatic play props; plan small group projects; take trips and walks in the neighborhood; eat family-style meals.

2. Answer should include methods of observation and assessment and specific ways teacher promotes skills.

3. Possible responses include: start or join a conversation by saying something to another person and wait for a response; take turns speaking when the other person has finished; look and listen to the person speaking; ask if you don't understand what someone has said; let the other person know that you are leaving the conversation.

4. Possible responses include: talk to children about how things feel, taste and smell; ask open-ended questions; name things; use full and complete sentences that describe details; take time to talk about feelings; describe the specific characteristics of objects or actions.

5. An appropriate book would have a simple plot, colorful illustrations, lots of repetition, rhymes, and/or nonsense words.

6. An appropriate book would have an imaginative story, colorful, detailed illustrations, a plot children can follow, humorous characters and events, and/or a story that extends children's understanding of the world around them.

<u>Matching</u>
7.
a. 2
b. 4
c. 3
d. 1

<u>Multiple Choice</u>
8. a
9. c
10. b
11. c

Module 7: Creativity

<u>Short Answers</u>

1. Answers may vary but should include: trying things and doing things in new ways; exploring , experimenting, and doing open-ended activities; and using different materials.

2. Answer should describe a specific activity with music and movement and provide sufficient detail on how it promotes creativity.

3. Possible responses include: paint, fingerpaint, playdough, building materials, clay, paste or glue, fabrics, scissors, sponge rollers, crayons.

4. Answer should include description of what was done and why it was creative.

5. Possible responses include: drums, cymbals, kazoos, hand bells, clackers, triangles, tambourines, xylophones, maracas.

<u>Matching</u>
6.
a. 2
b. 1
c. 4
d. 3

<u>Multiple Choice</u>
7. d
8. c
9. d
10. c

Module 8: Self

<u>Short Answers</u>

1. Answers may vary but should include sense of worth and self-confidence. These characteristics are necessary in school and in life.

2. Possible responses include: communicate frequently with children's families; observe children regularly; ask colleagues or trainer to observe children; note the kinds of activities children like; get to know your own style and preferences.

3. Answers may vary but should include something about materials, furniture, the daily schedule, and activities reflecting children's interests and abilities and making children feel included.

4. Possible responses include: talk with children about their parents during the day; listen to children as they express their feelings; make the environment as home-like as possible; encourage children to participate in activities to gain sense of competence and independence; involve children in daily routines and activities.

5. Possible responses include:
    <u>a</u>. listening carefully to determine what the child is saying
    <u>b</u>. responding so the child knows he or she is understood and respected

6. Answers may vary but should give specific examples that show how their own self-esteem affects the relationships with children in the program.

<u>Matching</u>
7.
a. 3
b. 4
c. 2
d. 1

<u>Multiple Choice</u>
8. c
9. c
10. b
11. b

Module 9: Social

<u>Short Answers</u>

1. Possible responses include: observe; establish a connection with the child; help children find good friends; organize small group activities in which the child can become involved; offer assistance only when necessary; know the interests of the child and build activities around those interests.

2. Possible responses include: help the child understand the consequences of his or her actions; redirect the child's anger; help the child develop ways to achieve goals without aggression; spend time alone with the child after he or she no longer exhibits aggressive behavior.

3. Possible responses include: show empathy; show generosity; help others; plan group activities that emphasize cooperation; help children learn how to talk about their feelings; read books on friendship and helpfulness.

4. Answers should give details on how the program supports children's social development.

5. Possible responses include: refer to children in their role names; model playful behaviors yourself; reinforce positive social behaviors as you observe them; help children get started, then step back; remind children of classroom rules within the context of play; engage them in conversation.

Matching
6.
a. 2
b. 1
c. 3
d. 4

Multiple Choice
7. b
8. c
9. d
10. c

Module 10: Guidance

Short Answers

1. Punishment is controlling children's behavior through fear or retaliation; discipline is guiding and directing children toward acceptable behavior. Discipline is positive in its effect; punishment does not lead to changes in behavior.

2. Possible responses include:
   a. "Do you need help putting your coat on? I'll show you a quick way to try."
   b. "Your mother will be here soon, just as she does every day around this time. Get your things so you'll be ready when she comes."

3. Possible responses include: reinforce children's positive behaviors; help children solve their own problems; anticipate problems and plan ways to avoid them; tell children what they can do; be polite to children; encourage children to move when they are restless; respond to behavior without labeling child.

4. Possible responses include: does the child have a medical or physical condition? Is the child getting enough attention? Is the child bored or understimulated? Is the child frustrated or discouraged? Did I give the child enough instruction on what is expected?

5. Answers may vary but should include details of the behavior and list specific details of how teacher responded.

Matching
6.
a. 3
b. 4
c. 2
d. 1

Multiple Choice
7. c
8. b
9. c
10. d

Module 11: Families

Short Answers

1. Possible responses include: health and growth history; temperament; interest; abilities; relationships with other family members; favorite activities at home; food preferences and allergies; reactions to certain situations; how best comforted.

2. Possible responses include: favorite interest areas and materials; what the child does at the program during the day; what challenges and kinds of activities the child enjoys; how the child reacts to changes in the environment; the child's social abilities at the program; teacher observations of the child's cognitive abilities and progress.

3. Answers should include description of what teacher finds rewarding and give reason(s) why.

4. Possible responses include: message box or folder for parents, parent bulletin board, newsletter, parent handbook, family journals, family photo board, weekly notes to parents.

5. Possible responses include: having parent orientations, family dinners, or family movie nights; holding weekend or evening workshops or seminars for parents; sending home a wish list for classroom materials; inviting parents to be book reviewers; establishing a parent corner.

6. Possible responses include:
a. ask parents about convenient days and times to meet; let parents know purpose of conference; ask parents to think of questions they may have and topics they would like to discuss; review and organize observation notes; ask colleagues to share information; collect samples of children's work; complete a planning form; role-play with a colleague to practice.
b. establish a relaxed and comfortable tone; explain how conference will proceed; provide opportunities for parents to ask questions and provide input; discuss all areas of child development; listen carefully and pay attention to parent's reactions; begin and end with positive statement about your relationship with child.

Multiple Choice
7. c
8. c
9. c
10. a

True/False
11. T
12. F-Teachers should always ask parents about their children's interests.
13. F-Both parents and teachers know a lot about a child.
14. T

Module 12: Program Management

Short Answers

1. Answers should include specific policies or procedures followed, such as recording daily attendance, meeting and greeting parents as they arrive.

2. Possible responses include: determine children's interests, strengths, and needs; plan an individualized program; document a child's progress; address a challenging behavior; report children's progress to parents and specialists; evaluate the program.

3. A portfolio, which consists of a child's work samples, provides concrete evidence of what a child can do. It also gives a balanced picture of a child's development.

4. See page 273 of Volume II for specific strategies.

5. Possible responses include: group time activities, small group activities, outdoor activities, changes to the environment, long-term studies.

6. Possible responses include: fine motor skills, gross motor skills, self-help skills, social skills, creativity, problem-solving skills, cooperative play, self-discipline, self-confidence, literacy skills.

Multiple Choice
7. b
8. c
9. c
10. c
11. b

True /False
12. F-It is best for several people to observe a child to confirm accuracy.
13. T
14. F-Planning is crucial to individualizing.
15. F-Evaluation is the last step in the planning process.
16. T
17. F-It is necessary to work as a team when planning a program so that everyone has the same goals and objectives.

Module 13: Professionalism

<u>Short Answers</u>

1. A professional is a person who uses specialized knowledge and skills to do a job or provide a service. Most will consider themselves professionals because their work requires specific knowledge and skills.

2. Answers should state that there is always new information to be learned, it is affirming, and it renews interest in the profession.

3. Possible responses include: join professional organizations; read books and articles; attend workshops and conferences;, keep a journal; use the Internet; network with colleagues.

4. Answers should reflect content of module.

<u>Multiple Choice</u>
5. a
6. c
7. b
8. b

<u>True/False</u>
9   T
10. F-Working with preschool children is a real profession.
11. F-It is a teacher's professional responsibility to speak out against inappropriate program practices.
12. F-Maintaining confidentiality about families extends beyond the program.

Appendix C

Tracking Forms

Individual Tracking Form

Name: _____

Indicate Date Completed

Module	Over-view	Pre-Training Assess-ment	L.A. I	L.A. II	L.A. III	L.A. IV	L.A. V	L.A. VI	Know-ledge Assess-ment	Compe-tency Assess-ment	Trainer Sign-off
Orientation	X	X	X	X	X	X	X	X	X	X	
1. Safe								X			
2. Healthy											
3. Learning Environment											
4. Physical								X			
5. Cognitive											
6. Communication								X			
7. Creative								X			
8. Self								X			
9. Social								X			
10. Guidance											
11. Families								X			
12. Program Management								X			
13. Professionalism								X		X	

Program Tracking Form

Modules

Teachers	OR		1		2		3		4		5		6		7		8		9		10		11		12		13	
	B	C	B	C	B	C	B	C	B	C	B	C	B	C	B	C	B	C	B	C	B	C	B	C	B	C	B	C

Legend

Modules:

OR-Orientation	4-Physical	8-Self
1-Safe	5-Cognitive	9-Social
2-Healthy	6-Communication	10-Guidance
3-Learning Environment	7-Creative	11-Families
		12-Program Management
		13-Professionalism

B- Begun
C- Completed

209

Appendix D

Training Record

Training Record

Name: _____   Program: _____

Topic	Date(s)	Hours	Type of Training (conference, course, workshop, observation/feedback)	Agency Providing Training	Signature of Trainer

Appendix E

Certificate of Completion

CERTIFICATE of COMPLETION

AWARDED TO

_____

for completion of _____ hours of training

on *Caring for Preschool Children, 2nd Edition*

_____ 199 ___

Verification of Training may be obtained from:

Agency Sponsoring Training: _____

Sponsor's Address: _____

City/State/Zip: _____

Sponsor's Phone Number: ( ) _____

_____
(Trainer's Signature)

Appendix F

Publishers and Distributors of Resources

Publishers and Distributors of Resources

The Orientation to *Caring for Preschool Children* includes a bibliography of recommended resources for early childhood professionals. Publishers and distributors of these resources are listed below.

American Public Health Association
1015 Fifteenth Street, NW
Washington, DC 20005
202-789-5600

American Academy of Pediatrics
141 Northwest Point Boulevard
Elk Grove Village, IL 60009
847-228-5005

Bantam Books
201 E. 50th Street
New York, NY 10022
212-751-2600

Bright Ring Publishing
P. O. Box 31338
Bellingham, WA 98228
206-734-1601

Centers for Disease Control
1600 Clifton Road, NE
Atlanta, GA 30333
404-639-3311

Crown Publishers
201 East 50th St.
New York, NY 10022
212-751-2600

David S. Lake Publishers
2113 Creekwood Drive
Fort Collins, CO 80525
303-224-4845

Delmar Publishers, Inc.
P. O. Box 15015
Albany, NY 12205-5015
518-464-3500
800-347-7707

DMC Publications
2113 Creekwood Drive
Fort Collins, CO 80525
303-224-4845

Dolphin Books
Doubleday and Company
1540 Broadway
New York, NY 10036-4094
212-782-8200

Early Educators Press
P. O. Box 1177
Lake Alfred, FL 33850
813-956-1569

Educational Resources Information Center (ERIC) Clearinghouse on Elementary and Early Childhood Education
University of Illinois
805 West Pennsylvania Avenue
Urbana, IL 61801-4897
800-583-4135

Exchange Press, Inc.
P. O. Box 2890
Redmond, WA 98073
206-883-9394

The Free Press
866 3rd Avenue
New York, NY 10022
212-702-2000

Glencoe Macmilllan/McGraw-Hill
936 Eastwind Drive
Westerville, OH 43081-3374
614-890-1111
800-848-1567

Gryphon House, Inc.
P. O. Box 207
Beltsville, MD 20704-0207
301-595-9500
800-638-0928

High/Scope Press
600 North River St.
Ypsilanti, MI 48198
313-485-2000

The Hanen Centre
252 Bloor Street West, Room 390
Toronto, Ontario M5S 1V5
416-921-1073

International Reading Association
800 Barksdale Road
P. O. Box 8139
Newark, DE 19714
302-731-1600

Little, Brown and Company
1271 Avenue of the Americas
New York, NY 10020
212-522-8700
800-759-0l90

National Association for the Education of Young Children
1509 16th Street, NW
Washington, DC 20036-1426
202-232-8777
800-424-2460

R & E Research Associates
468 Auzerais Avenue, Suite A
San Jose, CA 95126
408-977-0691

Redleaf Press
450 North Syndicate, Suite 5
St. Paul, MN 55104-9951
612-641-0305
800-423-8309

Southern Early Childhood Association (SECA)
P. O. Box 56130
Little Rock, AK 72215-6130
501-663-0353

Syracuse University Press
Syracuse, NY 13210
315-433-2597

Teachers College Press
Teachers College
Columbia University
New York, NY 10027
800-575-6566

Teaching Strategies, Inc.
P. O. Box 42243
Washington, DC 20015
202-362-7543
800-637-3652

TelShare Publishing Company, Inc.
24 Breakwater Drive
Chelsea, MA 02150
617-834-8774
800-343-9707

Turn-the-Page Press
203 Baldwin Avenue
Roseville, CA 95678
916-786-8756

Williamson Publishing
Church Hill Road, P. O. Box 185
Charlotte, VT 05445
802-425-2102
800-234-8791

NOTES

NOTES

NOTES

NOTES

NOTES

NOTES

NOTES

NOTES

NOTES

NOTES

NOTES

NOTES

NOTES

NOTES